Dr. Ben's Practical
Managing Self, Family, Relationships,
Work, and Friendships

TOOLS TO
THRIVE, NOT
JUST SURVIVE

Ben Accomando, Ph.D.

Print ISBN: 978-1-7348915-1-5

eBook ISBN: 978-1-7343332-9-9

This book is dedicated to all the brilliant psychological researchers and writers and all my patients for teaching me all that I know and all that I don't know about human nature.

CONTENTS

PREFACE

What Is My Vision for This Book?

After working for forty years as a clinical psychologist, I wanted to write a book dealing with three different areas of mental wellness that affect a large segment of the population. First, I wanted to educate the general population about mental illness and the treatments available. Second, I wanted to outline the destructive patterns that often result from irrational thinking, extreme emotions, and hostile behavior, and provide common-sense solutions to these problems. Third, I wanted to focus on the Five Systems of life, list the most common difficulties that people experience with them, and offer practical solutions to resolve them.

Why Write This Book?

First of all, after a comprehensive search of psychological self-help books, I found that most of them focus on one particular mental illness or personal problem in lengthy detail. I wanted to focus on the most common mental illnesses that people experience, offer a summary explanation and the services available for each, and provide practical solutions.

Second, unlike the typical self-help book, I wanted this book to be short, devoid of psychological jargon, and simply written. Many people who read self-help books tell me that the main points in the book could be easily summarized in fewer than five pages. They admit that they usually lose interest fairly quickly, and seldom finish reading the whole book.

Third, I wanted this book to be more comprehensive, and focus on the different systems that we, as human beings, deal and interact with daily in our lives, which include problems within: the family, romantic relationships, friendships and social life, work, and the many levels and complications within the individual "self."

Fourth, contrary to the common complaint that mental health professionals do not offer their patients reasonable solutions for their problems, I wanted to offer readers practical and common-sense solutions. During my years as a professional, I have discovered that most of the time my patients were eager to resolve their problems, and eagerly sought solutions because they were stuck in a cycle of sameness, doing the same things over and over.

Fifth, as I have done in dealing with my patients over the years, I wanted to challenge everyone reading this book to take full responsibility for their thoughts, emotions, and behaviors, rather than repeating the same unhealthy patterns and blaming the world for the results.

Who Can Use This Book?

I believe that the information provided in this book can be quite useful to anyone who wants basic knowledge on mental illnesses and the services available to treat them; needs better skills in managing the ups and downs of life; and seeks some practical solutions to their problems. I do believe that most people would be able to get much of this knowledge and insight if they were to seek the services of a mental health professional. Many never do, though.

In my experience treating people from all walks of life, I have been convinced that most people remain too uncomfortable to admit that they need the services of a mental health professional to deal with their problems. Many people are not very invested in seeking professional help, or are simply unwilling to do so, due to the many myths and negative biases connected to seeking counseling services, such as, "I'm not crazy!"

I believe that many people will be a lot more comfortable reading this book in the privacy of their own home, and perhaps will be more willing to challenge themselves and learn to confront their problems more honestly that way. I cannot imagine why anyone would not want to take advantage of the insight, education, and practical solutions provided by a mental health professional with more than forty years of experience. It's a great bargain!

How the Book Works

This book is presented in five sections. Each of these sections focuses on the most common problems that the majority of the population experiences in one or more of the following Five Systems of life: Self; Family; Romantic Relationships; Career; and Friendships. Each section addresses a list of specific problems followed by practical, bullet-point suggestions to be considered in trying to resolve them.

Part I focuses on the Individual and addresses self-identity. It also focuses on the difficulties and misconceptions that many individuals create and/or struggle with by the way they manage their thinking, emotions, and behavior.

The purpose of **Part II** is to discuss the importance, benefits, and difficulties involving the family of origin, the nuclear family, and the extended family. This section also includes detail on parenting problems and solutions.

The dynamics of a romantic partnership, from dating to divorce, are discussed in **Part III**. This section addresses methods of developing, improving, or more effectively dismantling relationships with the least

Part IV discusses the nuts and bolts of how to objectively evaluate your natural and learned skills, how to better prepare for a more appropriate selection of a career, and ultimately, how to succeed in achieving a more successful and satisfying career.

The importance and the many benefits of close friendships, and the social skills needed to develop and maintain relationships in general, are discussed in **Part V**. The focus will be on how to develop, manage, and flourish in the important goal of being socially confident in relationships and in having and keeping great friends.

I think it's fair to assume that, at one time or another, we all will have some difficulties in each of these five areas of our lives. It's also a fair assumption that when in the midst of these problems, we will often be confused and even irrational in our thoughts or actions. It's important to expect that these difficulties will come and to be careful not to think that we are being singled out by fate, that these "bad things only happen to me." Let's be realistic—no one is that special, and we all get our share of life's problems. Emotionally healthy individuals accept this fact.

How to Use This Book: A Note of Caution

The information in this book is not designed to offer professional advice on any and all mental illnesses and personal problems, nor should it be considered a substitute for psychological counseling provided by a qualified mental health professional. Instead, the descriptions of the general difficulties presented here, and the solutions offered, should be viewed as possible options to consider when dealing with these difficulties. I recommend that you seek the services of a qualified mental health professional if and when you experience significant mental illness and/or severe difficulties in managing your life.

Above All Else...

I hope that you use this book to face the parts of yourself that need improvement and growth with total honesty. I hope that you work hard at being responsible for yourself and for those in your life whom you love. Most of all, I hope that you avoid the "blame game," regardless of the pain in your life, and accept the reality that you are an adult and, therefore, fully responsible for your thoughts, emotions, and behavior.

I have learned that some suggestions can be very helpful for one person, but totally useless in helping someone else. I have also learned that I will never learn enough about us human beings to fully understand all our subtle complexities. But I offer you this book in the hope that some of these ideas will improve your quality of life and offer you some peace!

PART I

The Individual "Self":
From Self-Identity to
Self-Actualization

chapter one

SELF

> "We are what we pretend to be, so we must be careful
> about what we pretend to be."
> — Kurt Vonnegut

A Few Thoughts on the Subject of "Self"

We are ultimately a combination of our genetic predispositions and the influences from the environment in which we are born and raised. There have been many arguments over the years about the influences of "nature" versus "nurture," without achieving a consensus. Much of our personality results from what we inherit from our parents, and most of these predispositions are often unchangeable. But we can moderate or influence our personalities significantly over time.

Moreover, how we ultimately develop into adulthood is significantly influenced by our family's philosophies, attitudes, parenting styles, and history in general. We know that we cannot fully develop our own personality until the age of thirteen or later, allowing for major influence from our families. Values practiced by most family members, especially our parents, are usually taken on and practiced by us as well as we grow into adulthood.

Additional influences affecting our development include our social system, important people in our lives, and life experiences that we may have gone through, either negative or positive, during our development.

Finally, psychological, physiological, environmental, and emotional imbalances that can be influenced by the extremity of our thoughts, emotions, and behaviors ultimately play a major role in our decision making and quality of life.

All of these influences will ultimately dictate the type, quality, peacefulness, and volatility of our lives. That includes how we manage our relationships with family, friends, and significant others; the way we approach our careers; and the way we view, think, feel, and treat ourselves.

1. The Problem: Developing Your Own Identity

"Knowing yourself is the beginning of all wisdom."

— Aristotle

Your identity can be your own personal creation and can be molded by the powerful influences of your family, friends, and educators. Often, we are confused as to who we are or who we are supposed to be in trying to live up to everyone else's expectations. To eliminate the confusion and avoid becoming a chameleon, it is best at times to reject everyone's expectations of who you should be and develop your own ideal and personal identity. Yes, you can create your ideal self and strive to evolve into it every day!

Possible Solutions

- Think about what the "ideal you" would truly be like in your everyday thoughts, emotions, and actions.

- Choose a set of core values, philosophies, attitudes, and views to live by, and practice them daily.

- Define for yourself how this "ideal you" would think, feel, and act when dealing with family, romantic partners, friends, co-workers, and other influential people in your life.

- Practice daily all of the new values and attributes that you have selected for the "ideal you."

- Ask yourself at the end of every day how successfully you have practiced being the new you.

- Make a mental note on what to improve on the next day. Be honest in assessing your efforts, but do not be too critical of yourself. You are growing into your new you every day!

2. The Problem: Finding Your Internal Balance

While we have no direct control over what we feel, we can influence it by what we think and do. The mind is a powerful tool, and our thoughts can exaggerate and distort reality in either positive or negative ways. Similarly, our actions can have a positive or negative impact on our feelings and thoughts. Both our thoughts and our actions influence our emotions. So if you change what you think, you will change how you feel—which will change how you act! The reverse is also true. What you do leads to what you feel, which leads to what you think. Want to feel better? Think positive, stay in the moment, take positive action!

Possible Solutions

- Challenge your negative thoughts whenever you find yourself worrying about the future.

- Predict the best possible outcome in your mind when you have something important coming up in the future.

- Select, remember, and talk about only the best memories from your past, and let bad memories be forgotten.

- Focus on the present as much as possible, while having a general direction for the future. Always avoid thinking and obsessing about bad situations in the past.

- Ask yourself, whenever you are worrying about something, "Does worrying about this problem help?"

- Try to convince yourself to challenge the reality of the fearful, negative, or gloomy thoughts that your mind may create and try to convince you are true.

3. The Problem: Keeping Life Simple

I believe that people often complicate life unnecessarily. At times, there is confusion between an opinion and a fact. The problem is further complicated by the illusion that we can actually control things. Keeping life simple requires that we honestly answer the following three questions when faced with a problem:

A. What do I want?

B. Is what I want under my control?

C. Am I willing to accept the consequences of my actions?

Remember, your actions are totally under your control, and you have to be willing to face their consequences. You can do anything you want if you are willing to pay the consequences!

Possible Solutions

- Question yourself honestly whether what you want is truly under your control—don't assume.

- Evaluate all the emotional, financial, and social costs of getting what you want.

- Assess your expectations with a logical and reasonable mindset before assuming or acting.

- Realize that statements like "I want my wife/husband to..." refer to things that are not in your control.

- Assess the other person's point of view before concluding that he or she is wrong.

- Practice being practical, rather than emotional and unreasonable, in your expectations.

4. The Problem: Managing Your Emotions

Everyone is entitled to feel the full intensity of every emotion, without exception. However, remember that healthy people don't arbitrarily act on their emotions. Instead, regardless of how we feel, we must behave logically and reasonably, with a clear goal in mind. Many people conclude that because they are upset, they are free to act however they want. The truth is that adults are expected to be respectful and reasonable, regardless of how they feel.

Possible Solutions

- Think before you act, regardless of how upset you are at that moment.

- Focus on the solution to a problem rather than your feelings about the problem.

- Express your feelings when upset in an "I" statement, rather than in the accusing "you" tone.

- Count to ten slowly before you speak, at all times, especially when angry and frustrated.

- Evaluate the other person's intent rather than their actions before making a judgment.

- Always seek the most reasonable and logical solution for every problem you face in life.

5. The Problem: Facing Your Fears

Often, people seek counseling to find ways to eliminate fears or build more courage, confidence, or understanding. But confidence and bravery are usually the result of taking action, rather than of a discussion *about* an action. Confidence develops as the result of having taken action in spite of how insecure, scared, or uncomfortable we might have been. It is the doing, not the planning, that helps us face fears and gain confidence.

Possible Solutions

- Fear is often created by what we imagine will happen, not by the reality of what actually happens.

- Challenge your fears by doing something uncomfortable every day with resolution and a smile.

- Question all of the irrational thoughts, which are stopping you from doing what you need to do.

- Accept your discomfort as a normal reaction to the things you don't yet know.

- Recognize how strongly your mind can mislead you after you have gone through fearful experiences.

- Enjoy the great feeling of proving your fears wrong after you have successfully taken action.

6. The Problem: Finding the Answers Within

Very often we blame our partner, our job, the weather, our neighbors, and even our community for our misery. We convince ourselves and others that if only the situation were different, then our lives would be more satisfactory and we would be happier. Yes, upsetting things happen to everyone, and no, we are not exempt from them, but we can make any situation much better with the right attitude, more optimistic thinking, and a positive frame of mind. Most often, we generate our own internal turmoil rather than facing the situations that are in front of us.

Possible Solutions

- Ask yourself, "Am I overreacting?" whenever you find yourself worried over something.

- Review all the good things you have been blessed with in the recent past, rather than focusing on the negatives.

- When you are upset, list five things you can be thankful for.

- Compare your life with others who have it much worse than you.

- Choose to go for a brisk walk, take some deep breaths, and appreciate the beauty around you.

- Ask yourself, "Will what just happened really make a difference six months from now?"

7. The Problem: Managing Your Mental Health

At times, mental illness is the result of genes or some physiological anomaly. Most often, however, mental illness is the result of an individual's distorted thinking, extreme emotions, and destructive behavior. Unfortunately, those who struggle with mental illness are usually unaware of it, too fearful to face it, or too deep into it to be aware of what they can do to help themselves. I truly believe that the majority of the mental disorders from which the general population suffers can be prevented or easily treated with a better understanding of the issues and professional help when truly needed.

Possible Solutions

- Review your sleep, eating, relaxation, and socialization patterns for possible problems.

- Listen carefully to those who love you when they are worried about you.

- Pay attention to any mood shifts, aberrant thoughts, or strange behaviors you may be experiencing.

- Recognize any signs of anxiety, panic, fear, depression, or abnormal functioning and get help.

- Notice any change or reduction in your level of functioning at work, home, or any other areas of life.

- Seek professional help if you recognize any of the problems above. Do not ignore them too long.

8. The Problem: Accepting the Realities of Life

Many people, when confronted with life's difficulties, often ask the question, "Why me?" They are truly convinced that a normal life should equal a life without problems. I often sarcastically respond, "I'm curious, what is it about you that makes you so special that you should be exempt from life's struggles?" No one is exempt from life's problems, and everyone should expect their share of them along the way. When you are not experiencing many struggles, try to enjoy these precious times, knowing and accepting that you will have difficulties coming in the future.

Possible Solutions

- Compare your difficulties with those of ten other people you know and see how much you have in common.

- Review honestly how many people you know who have a problem-free life.

- Question your assumption that a normal life equals a problem-free life.

- Evaluate your problems on a scale of 1 to 100, where 1 equals a disaster and 100 equals perfection.

- Prioritize what is most important to you, and compare that with the problems you face.

9. The Problem: Accepting That You Don't Know

At times, we can all be arrogant enough to believe that what we think is the unquestionable truth. Some people tend to practice this attitude most of the time, remaining rigid in their position, convinced that they are right. Unfortunately, people with this attitude fail to learn valuable lessons while going through life proud of their "knowledge." The same people often confuse an opinion with a fact. I love the expression, "We don't know what we don't know"!

Possible Solutions

- Always be open to learning things beyond your own views on any subject.

- Question whether you actually gave serious thought to the other person's point of view.

- Ask yourself what you could actually learn from the other person's logic and way of thinking.

- Review the reasons why being wrong is ultimately so difficult for you to accept most of the time.

- Take the other person's position and come up with a few arguments as to why they might be right.

- Seriously consider the possibility that sometimes you really "don't know what you don't know."

10. The Problem: Being Realistic in Your Expectations

Most of us have expectations about people in our lives, individuals in our community, and even the leaders who run our country. Unfortunately, the idea that we are also different from one another seems to escape many people's minds. We give ourselves the right to criticize someone for their attitude or actions as long as we conclude that our standard for their behavior is reasonable. We may believe that we are entitled to set the bar for what is acceptable, and demand that others live up to it. We must consider that reasonableness as well as fairness are subjective concepts. Others are not necessarily wrong in what they think and do; they might just be different.

Possible Solutions

- Question whether what you think is "reasonable" is similar to what you would do in a given situation.

- Evaluate whether you have the right to judge someone's actions because you don't approve of them.

- Assess honestly whether your way should always be everyone else's way of handling things.

- Recognize that the only realistic choice that is under your control is whether you accept the other person in your life.

- Evaluate whether your position may be too rigid and/or demanding.

- Think of the possibility that you are carrying around a "book of rules" and demanding that everyone follow them.

11. The Problem: Separating Who You Are from What You Do

Often, we identify ourselves and are judged by others on the basis of the job we have, the amount of money we make, or even how physically attractive we are. Sadly, our sense of worth and individuality may be lost in the labels we are given. Despite the advantages good-looking people may receive in life, the healthiest way to build a sense of self is from the inside out, rather than from the outside in.

Possible Solutions

- Ask yourself how often you ask someone you just met, "So what do you do?"

- Review your thoughts about yourself and question how you define who you are.

- Question whether you treat people you know differently based on whether they are wealthy or a little different than others.

- Ask yourself in whose company you feel insecure about yourself, and in whose company you feel confident.

- Remember that until you accept who you are, you will be at the mercy of others to define yourself.

12. The Problem: Believing You Know Yourself

Most people believe that no one knows them better than they know themselves. But not many of us truly know ourselves well. We may also think that we know what others think of us, and then be blindsided by unusual reactions or criticism we get from them. Most of us don't have the necessary self-awareness to know what others think of us. So ultimately, we are often wrong about what we think of ourselves, and wrong about what other people think of us as well. We need to dig in and look at ourselves, with honesty and humility, and then listen to others.

Possible Solutions

- Seek accurate knowledge about yourself from those you trust and those who love you.

- Open yourself up and accept constructive criticism designed to teach you more about yourself.

- Learn to be more introspective and honestly question your thoughts, emotions, and actions.

- Accept the truths you discover from self-search; this will help you grow and be healthier.

- Remember that being healthy requires internal and external checks and balances, and input from within and without.

- Ask others for details and suggestions when you are getting feedback about yourself, no matter how painful it might be.

13. The Problem: Looking to Solve Your Problems

Very often people struggling with problems seek help from family, friends, and professionals. I have found that many people seek my help with the goal of feeling better, and they may be disappointed when I explain that counseling can be difficult and at times painful. The role of a therapist is to challenge the client's irrational thoughts, question the extremes in their emotions, and question their logic in explaining their destructive behavior. The responsibility of the client is to consider and apply the necessary suggestions that are designed to generate internal and external changes, regardless of the discomfort involved. Solving problems is difficult; talking may make you feel better for a short time, but it won't solve the problem. Therefore, once you learn something important, take action and make changes.

Possible Solutions

- Think about the solution the helper has offered, rather than how you feel after the discussion.

- Recognize that the guidance offered is designed to help you grow.

- Practice whatever behaviors or thoughts have been offered to you to get the solutions you want.

- Recognize that "feeling better" is based on the result of the changes, rather than just talking about them.

- Remember that seeking help often translates into learning something that you did not know or necessarily want to hear.

- Know that making changes is difficult for everyone, and you are not exempt from life's struggles and difficulties.

14. The Problem: Being Honest, Above All Else

Perhaps we say things to make ourselves feel better for the moment, or have others see us in a better light. Perhaps we need scapegoats to compensate for our lack of effort, our limitations, or even our ignorance. Perhaps we have not yet begun the self-actualization process, so our need to lie makes us behave as social chameleons according to the situation. However, in order to ultimately live an honorable, comfortable, and internally peaceful life, we have to try very hard to be honest with ourselves and others.

- Take responsibility for your screw-ups and contributions to any problem.

- Accept that it is perfectly acceptable to be imperfect, as long as you try.

- Recognize that the discomfort you feel after you have lied is an important message from your conscience.

- Remember that it takes a strong person to confront and admit their flaws and weaknesses.

- Don't blame your parents, your upbringing, your disabilities, or the world for your attitude and actions. You are responsible for what you do.

- Remember Shakespeare's "This above all: to thine own self be true…"

15. The Problem: Knowing Your Sense of Purpose

We need to be very careful not to confuse a life that is busy with one that is purposeful. Our lives seem to be getting faster and faster every day, although it is often difficult to account for any valuable achievement. With many people addicted to their smartphones and rushing through high-pressure careers, finding time to reflect can be difficult. Clearly, committing to meaningful, long-term goals becomes more difficult when we keep a busy life, which can easily lead to loss of interest, restlessness, and boredom. A truly satisfying life requires a passionate and clear sense of purpose, which drives our desires daily and usually involves helping others in some way.

- Define with clarity the most important things that you do every day in your life.

- Evaluate honestly: How important and satisfying are those things that you have on your daily schedule?

- Question yourself: How well do you challenge your intelligence and other skills in your daily life?

- Be honest with yourself: Do you wake up looking forward to something challenging and meaningful every day?

- Question yourself: Does what you are doing compare well with what you would truly like to do?

- Identify the passion inside you; plan to go after those things with all your heart as soon as possible.

16. The Problem: Defining Your Personal Freedom

Whenever we spend time trying to get other people to do what they don't want to do, or resist others who are trying to get us to do something we don't want to do, we infringe on our sense of mutual freedom. Once we recognize and accept that the only thing we can actually control is ourselves, we start to redefine our personal freedom. Similarly, we need to recognize that when we try to convince others to do something against their wishes, we are trying to violate their personal freedom. Yes, the ultimate statement of freedom is, "Do what you want to do, don't do what you don't want to do, and take responsibility for the consequences that follow."

Possible Solutions

- Recognize that when you give an ultimatum to someone, you're redefining both your and their freedom.

- Know that, when all is said and done, no one can make you do anything you don't want to do. There are always choices, and those choices always have consequences.

- Don't blame others for things that you agree to do or not do; you decided, and you need to accept the consequences of your decision.

- Whether to comply with someone else's demands is ultimately still your choice.

- Deciding to be free and in charge of your own thoughts, emotions, and behaviors, whether good or bad, usually has consequences.

- Creating your own path, even if less traveled than others' paths, does not mean you are lost. It might set you free to be you.

17. The Problem: Accepting That Most Problems Are Relationship-Related

Regardless of how we try to understand our unhappiness, the main reasons for it are usually important relationships in our lives that are not working out to our satisfaction. Even problems that don't seem to be about relationships, like a general sense of stress, may actually be about the people in our lives. Strangely, we often ignore these relationship problems and instead blame our struggles on other problems in our lives. Sooner or later, though, we must face the real sources and confront them honestly.

Possible Solutions

- Face reality with honesty to understand what you are really unhappy about in your life.

- Remember that connecting with people who are important in your life usually offers the greatest satisfaction.

- Don't assume that you can always solve your problems, but know that in ignoring them, you will never have the oppor-tunity to solve anything.

- Think about your struggles, and you will usually identify the source to be a relationship that is important to you.

- Understand that you cannot force anyone to love or stop loving you or anyone else.

- Allocate more time and energy to your relationships than anything else in life.

18. The Problem: Getting Stuck in the Past

Lao Tzu, a Chinese philosopher, said, "If you are depressed, you're living in the past. If you are anxious, you're living in the future. If you are at peace, you're living in the present." Wisdom dictates that revisiting the painful past can offer us little knowledge about what we need to focus on today. The past will only make us more upset or depressed and keep us prisoners of situations that we cannot do any-thing about. Healthier goals would be to focus on doing the best we can to correct our present areas of difficulty, and letting the painful past be forgotten.

Possible Solutions

- Look to the past and search for happy memories and valu-able lessons that you have learned and can apply to your life today.

- Know that bringing up the negatives and past hurts, espe-cially in your romantic relationships, can only cause more conflict and disagreements in the present.

- Recognize that if you keep reviewing the past, you will give power to it and be held prisoner by it.

- Remember that thinking that you must revisit the past before dealing with the present is truly faulty logic.

- Remember that our minds work to erase the memories of the painful past; don't dig them up again unnecessarily.

- Freedom is best achieved by staying in the moment and dealing only with the present problems and pleasures.

19. The Problem: Recognizing That We May Choose Our Misery

Over the years I have seen thousands of people who present their struggles in terms of, "I am suffering from…" They never fully identified their difficulties as, to some degree, a personal choice that they made. People would often say "I suffer from depression" or "I suffer from anxiety" or "I am really anxious and depressed." I truly believe that if they viewed their suffering in terms of, "I choose to be depressed; I choose to be anxious; I choose to think in helpless ways," then they would feel a much greater sense of control and could more easily set themselves free. Truly, with only some minimal exceptions, we can choose to eliminate a lot of the self-imposed suffering and problems we face.

Possible Solutions

- Freedom is ultimately based on the understanding that we make our own choices in what we think, feel, and do.

- Remember that you have total control over your thoughts and behaviors at all times.

- Thinking that things "happen" to you makes you a prisoner of the external powers in life, taking away your power to decide.

- Feelings cannot be directly controlled, but you clearly can control them based on how you act or think about things.

- Recognize that in accepting that you have choices, you will believe that you are the master of your destiny.

- Control becomes an illusion when you allow your happiness to be someone else's responsibility.

20. The Problem: Identifying and Satisfying Your Needs

We are driven by needs that, sooner or later, must be satisfied: among them are survival, power, freedom, love, and fun. We strive to fulfill these needs, in one form or another, every day of our lives. While they can be postponed, they will have to be satisfied, and can only be satisfied by us and no one else. Sometimes we assume that other people can satisfy these needs for us and, ultimately, we will be disappointed. Sometimes we attempt to satisfy other people's needs and lose ourselves in an impossible task. In doing so, we lose ourselves and our freedom.

Possible Solutions

- Identify the image of the ideal in your mind for each of these needs and try to achieve it every day.

- Remember that you are your own master, responsible for satisfying your own needs; you must depend on only yourself to work toward these ideals.

- Recognize that you cannot take responsibility for satisfying someone else's needs. You may want to give of yourself, but do so without expectations of reciprocity.

- Realize that if you take total responsibility for someone else's needs, you will ultimately fail both yourself and the other person.

- Remember that what you select as your ideal situation is usually what is most important to you, not to everyone else.

- Know that you are the only one who can decide when and how these needs will ever be satisfied.

21. The Problem: Managing Your Anger

Anger is one of the most damaging and difficult human emotions. In the past, it was popular to advise that one openly and freely express feelings of rage; "let it all hang out" was the common expression. Nowadays, such behavior is not only no longer acceptable; it can get one into physical confrontations or legal difficulties. The idea of "zero tolerance" is in force. Interestingly enough, the solution to managing anger was first suggested thousands of years ago by the Greek philosopher Epictetus, who said, "What disturbs people's minds is not events but their judgments on events." This philosophy was popularized in the 1970s by the development of Rational-Emotive Therapy. Most influential in this therapeutic approach was Albert Ellis, Ph.D., at his institute in New York City. He spoke about the idea of belief systems, which can fall into two categories, rational and irrational beliefs, and argued that our irrational beliefs about an event may have a strong and overwhelming influence over our responses. If we change our thoughts into rational beliefs, we then can change our responses and behaviors. I believe that we should expect—no, we should demand—that adults behave appropriately and respectfully toward other people, regardless of their feelings.

Possible Solutions

- Remember that as an adult, you are not entitled to act irrationally under any circumstances.

- Question whether you are about to overreact to a particular situation before you actually take an action.

- Think and challenge your first angry thoughts before taking a strong and irresponsible action.

- Recognize that rage is often the result of your irrational, exaggerated thoughts.

- Challenge yourself and take ten seconds before you react to a frustrating situation: be more practical!

- Demand of yourself to be reasonable at all times, regardless of the unreasonable circumstances you may be facing.

chapter two

MENTAL ILLNESS: FROM NORMALITY TO SCHIZOPHRENIA

"Out of suffering have emerged the strongest souls.
The most massive characters are seared with scars."

— Khalil Gibran

A Few Thoughts on Mental Illness

Mental illness is a complex phenomenon that can be difficult to diagnose and, at times, very difficult to treat as well. The best way to recognize mental illness is to observe how well or poorly an individual functions in the five systems of life: family, friends, romantic relationships, work, and identity. The main evidence of mental illness is when an individual shows distorted thinking, extreme emotions, and destructive behavior contrary to the rules and mores of the community in which that individual lives. One in four people in the world suffer from some type of mental disorder, ranging from mild to extreme.

Recognize that a diagnosis of mental illness is only a label, usually necessary so that there are some prescribed guidelines in place for treatment. A diagnosis is often required by health insurance companies for reimbursement for services provided by mental health professionals. Generally, mental illnesses fall into six to eight different categories, which may include:

- Anxiety disorders

- Mood disorders

- Eating disorders

- Personality disorders

- Substance abuse disorders

- Personality disorders

- Schizophrenia

- Dementia

There are a lot more subcategories of mental illness within each of the categories listed above. The sources of mental illness vary; some illnesses seem to be connected to family genes, while others may be connected to biological makeup of the individual. Some have been recognized as neurological deficits, and still others can originate from unhealthy struggles within the systems of family, romantic relationships, friendships, work, and identity.

If you're wondering whether you (or someone you know) suffer from a mental illness, think about the questions below. Answer yes if these difficulties have been going on for at least a few months.

1. Have you noticed, or have others told you, that your thinking is irrational?

2. Have you noticed, or have others said to you, that often you are too emotional?

3. Do you recognize, or have you been told, that you have been acting destructively?

4. Do you find yourself overwhelmed, confused, or lost by even simple daily routines?

5.   Do you often struggle or find yourself in conflict with people in the family, friends, romantic partners, or co-workers?

If any of these problems have been going on for quite a while without any resolution, then it is strongly recommended to seek professional help.

22. The Problem: Utilizing Counseling Effectively

The question, "When is it time to go for counseling?" is difficult to answer directly, but I think it is useful to follow some general guidelines that will help you make the appropriate decision. How to go about finding an appropriate mental health professional also requires some careful thought and action on your part.

When you have decided that you need counseling, it is very important to follow certain steps and utilize the time effectively. The different professionals that offer mental health counseling include: psychologists, psychiatrists, social workers, and other counselors, including marriage and family therapists. Make sure that the professional you choose has some expertise in the areas that you are struggling with. Remember that talking about your difficulties is seldom the ultimate solution to them. Most likely, you need to consider doing something different than what you have been doing to help yourself. Once you have selected an appropriate professional for your difficulties, you should consider following these steps as an effective guideline to maximize your success.

- Don't wait too long to seek help when you are experiencing significant difficulties; these problems don't usually get better on their own.

- Reach out to a family doctor or a trusted and close family member to help you get the help you need if you don't know how to find a professional.

- Don't let the fear of being labeled "crazy" keep you from seeking professional help as soon as possible.

- No, you are not "crazy" if you are told that you need to take psychotropic medication or undergo counseling.

- Make sure that you have the appropriate and qualified professional to help you help yourself and get better; try more than one if you're not satisfied.

- Don't panic if you don't feel better quickly; give yourself some time to improve and you will get better.

- Accept responsibility, don't blame others for your problems, and work at solving them rather than blaming others and feeling sorry for yourself.

- Don't go for counseling to complain; instead, utilize it effectively by following the insights and suggestions offered to solve your problems.

- Make a written list of the problems you want the therapist to help resolve, and share it with the therapist during the first session.

- Ask questions you believe are important. By the end of the first session, be clear about what you want to know and say you don't understand if you don't.

- During the session, write down ideas, insights, and suggestions offered so that you can remember them.

- Assign yourself homework that you are going to work on based on the suggestions made, and make sure you do it over the following week.

23. The Problem: Managing Anxiety

"Worry is like a rocking chair, it will give you something to do but it won't get you anywhere."

— Vance Havner

An anxiety disorder is an emotional, physiological, and behavioral reaction to an imbalance within our system when different parts of the brain are in disarray. There are ten different types of anxiety, but for simplicity's sake, only general information will be presented here. The reaction (anxiety) can vary in intensity and occur from time to time, usually when the body and/or mind are in distress. It is helpful to realize that an effective neural balance is necessary for healthy function. The command center of our body is our brain, and as such, our brain is responsible for anxiety. In managing our anxiety, the goal is to rebalance the brain so that all its systems can function properly. Without going into detail, it is useful to understand that there are certain chemicals in the brain that, when their levels are disrupted or shifted, generate changes, especially two particular chemicals: serotonin and norepinephrine. When these chemicals are in disarray, we can experience anxiety and depression. Thus, anxiety and depression are a chemical imbalance in the brain. More than 40 million people in this country suffer from anxiety, which is the most common mental health disorder in our population.

The most common symptoms of anxiety:

Physical symptoms: blushing, sweating, shaking, palpitations, difficulty breathing, chest pain, nausea, dizziness, tingling, increase in heart rate, physical weaknesses, stomach pain.

Distorted thoughts: fear of being judged, catastrophizing, predicting the worst possible scenario, assigning negative traits to oneself, focusing only on negative possibilities, being stuck in the "what if ?" of possible occurrences in the future, looking at things as all or none, self-blaming, being stuck in reviewing the past, regretting everything in life.

Emotions: guilt, perfectionism, confusion, panic, fear, worry, insecurity, negativity, avoidance, depression, worthlessness.

The Ideal Treatment Approach for Anxiety

The present available treatment for anxiety disorders includes psychological counseling, psychotropic medications, and the practice of techniques such as cognitive behavioral therapy, deep breathing exercises, physical exercise, relaxation techniques, reviewing the past for unhealthy parenting and the ultimate acceptance that managing anxiety is under your control.

Possible Solutions

- Don't ignore moderate anxiety or panic attacks; they are unlikely to stop on their own, so be sure to get psychological help or practice the techniques listed above.

- Know that you have control over what you think and do. Your thoughts may cause you to worry or be fearful unnecessarily, ultimately generating anxiety.

- Accept that you can control and redirect what you think at all times; therefore you can control whether or not you are going to get anxious.

- Realize that you have to drive "toward," not "away" from, your anxiety and fears to ultimately overcome them.

- Don't fixate on all the "what ifs" for any situation in the future; you cannot predict the future, and this will only generate anxiety.

- Recognize when "the tail is wagging the dog": when your anxiety is controlling you. That's the time to consider taking medication.

24. The Problem: Managing Mood Disorders

"The happiness of your life depends upon the quality of your thoughts."

— Marcus Aurelius

Mood disorders range from mild depression to severe bipolar disorder and can have debilitating effects. Again, only general information will be offered here, and it should be noted that many of the treatment approaches for mood disorders are similar to those described for anxiety disorders. Also, like anxiety, mood disorders are emotional, physiological, and behavioral reactions to an imbalance within one's system when different and complicated parts of the brain are in disarray. The sources of mood disorders may be biological factors, genetic vulnerabilities, environmental influences, or the negative impact of an individual's upbringing. Clinical depression varies from mild to severe, and it is not the same as grieving after the loss of a loved one or a personal crisis. The specific functions causing depression are beyond the scope of this book, although it is important to point out that the chemistry influencing it, as with an anxiety disorder, includes the serotonin, norepinephrine levels in the brain.

The most common symptoms of depression:

Emotional symptoms: low motivation, irritable mood, and anhedonia (the inability to feel pleasure).

Physiological symptoms: fatigue, lack of interest in the usual activities, increase or decrease in appetite, weight loss or gain, low energy, sleeping too little or too much, and psychomotor agitation or slowing.

Cognitive symptoms: hopelessness, difficulty making decisions, feeling of worthlessness, concentration impairment, rumination, pessimism, and excessive guilt.

Other symptoms: thoughts about dying, suicidal ideation, strong desire to get rid of the pain.

The Ideal Treatment Approach for Mood Disorders

The most comprehensive treatment approach for mood disorders includes psychological counseling to focus on the sources of the symptoms, psychotropic medication when symptoms are severe, and certain techniques that have been recognized in research as effective tools for reducing symptoms. For more severe mood disorders, like bipolar disorder I or II, it is almost always assumed that psychotropic medication will be prescribed as part of the treatment, and the patient needs to be closely monitored by both the psychiatrist and the treating psychologist. Severe mood disorders at times may require a more aggressive treatment approach, including Electroconvulsive Therapy (ECT) and hospitalization.

- Don't ignore the symptoms of mood disorders; they will eventually get worse without appropriate counseling, medication, and/or other proven techniques.

- Accept that if you been diagnosed with severe depression, you will need to take medication, at least for a while, until the depression has subsided.

- Realize that often you choose to be depressed by getting yourself stuck in gloomy thoughts. You can choose to help yourself by being more optimistic and positive about life in general.

- Know that managing depression is directly related to managing your thoughts and behaviors; yes, you can redirect your thoughts and change your behaviors.

- Accept that controlling depression and feeling better are mainly up to you by seeking appropriate help and accepting medication when necessary.

- Follow your doctor's recommendations and suggestions; don't fight them and allow your fears and negativity to take over.

25. The Problem: Managing Suicidal Thoughts

Suicide is on the rise in this country, especially among people in the age range of fifteen to twenty-four, and this is a very important subject that requires some insight and understanding. I believe that no suicide is ever justified, but that we have the right to do whatever we want with our lives, even terminate them if we so choose. I also believe that no one can ultimately stop a person who has made the decision to commit suicide. So the following information is being provided to those people who are only considering the idea of suicide, because they are looking for a method of eliminating their severe emotional pain and the powerful sense of helplessness driven by their unsuccessful efforts to resolve their difficulties.

Some of the underlying reasons for suicidal thoughts or acts may include: significant mental illness; emotional and physical pain; terminal illness; loneliness; substance abuse; a broken heart; traumatic experiences; financial crises; eating disorders; and bullying or social humiliation. Some people consider suicide as a way to express anger toward people very close to them.

Possible Solutions

- Remember that suicide is a permanent solution to a temporary problem, no matter how painful the problem happens to be.

- Recognize and accept that it is normal to feel sad, anxious, scared, and depressed at times; with appropriate help, things will get better.

- Don't allow your mind to make tragedies out of problems that could be managed with the right solutions.

- Accept the challenge and opportunity to build your strength and character through adversity.

- Don't judge yourself on what you have or what you do; judge yourself only on who you are, because that's the only thing that matters.

- Don't trap yourself in rigid and gloomy positions; widen your scope by opening your mind to different opportunities and different options.

Other Significant Mental Illnesses

Other mental illnesses that everyone should be aware of and recognize are summarized in this section. Again, I will only touch on some general features of these illnesses, but I want to be clear that this does not imply that they are not major problems requiring immediate psychological intervention, especially when severe behaviors are involved. I strongly recommend that if you, or anyone you know, are experiencing any of the following problems, you should seek help as quickly as possible. Unfortunately, some of these difficulties are not recognized or willingly acknowledged by the individuals who suffer from them. Psychological interventions usually take place in cases of emergency or when dictated by family members, doctors, or the law.

26. The Problem: Controlling Eating Disorders

Eating disorders are significant mental health problems in the United States that include anorexia, bulimia nervosa, and binge eating disorders. While there is significant attention on overeating in our society, obesity is not always identified as a mental health disorder. Unfortunately, eating disorders are often not detected because those who suffer from them are quite avoidant and secretive about it. Treatment of these disorders varies according to the level of severity and the type of disorder, but it is crucial to seek psychological treatment, especially for anorexia, which, when left untreated for a long time, can lead to death. Less common disorders that fall under this category include pica, rumination disorders, and avoidant/restrictive food intake disorders. Eating disorders can have a major negative impact on emotional and physiological health and often require treatment.

- Face the reality that your effort at manipulating food has little to do with food and all to do with a strong desire for control.

- Recognize that an eating disorder will ultimately affect your body as well as your mind, and can lead to permanent psychological and physical damage.

- Know that while you may believe being very skinny is beautiful, most other people see you as being physically ill.

- Bingeing and purging are dangerous activities that can cause damage to multiple parts of your body.

- Don't deny and dismiss people's concerns about your unhealthy eating behavior; instead, accept it and get help quickly.

Personality Disorders

> *"A little sincerity is a dangerous thing, and a great deal of it is absolutely fatal."*
>
> — Oscar Wilde

Personality disorders encompass a cluster of maladaptive disorders, usually identified by extreme negative behaviors that are pathological and destructive in nature. These disorders are often difficult or impossible to treat, and the individuals who suffer from them seldom, if ever, voluntarily seek treatment. Some of these disorders include (1) borderline personality disorder, (2) narcissistic personality disorder, (3) histrionic personality disorder, and (4) antisocial personality disorder.

1. Individuals who suffer from **Borderline Personality Disorder** have a self-defeating cycle of behavior and are driven by an unconscious fear of abandonment. Unfortunately, because of their extreme, intense, and negative behavior, others usually end up avoiding, rejecting, and ultimately abandoning them, and their greatest fear comes true.

It should be noted that solutions are being offered only to those who deal with borderline personalities rather than those who suffer from them. The reason for this decision is based on the reality that those people who are borderline seldom self identify themselves as the problem . I suggest, for those who recognize that they have a personality disorder, to seek competent psychological treatment.

Possible Solutions for Those Who Deal with Borderline Personalities

- Establish clear boundaries in your relationship with a borderline personality, and deny any unrealistic expectations of unhealthy intimacy.

- Take boundary violations seriously, including any threats of violence, verbal or physical, against you or others.

- Don't try to get them to get help or try to fix their problems for them. This will only generate anger in them.

- Pay close attention to your gut feelings of discomfort and fear, and quickly set boundaries and create distance.

- Don't argue with or criticize the borderline personality; respond matter-of-factly, and hold your ground and your position.

2. Individuals with **Narcissistic Personality Disorder** are driven by an unconscious fear of inferiority. Unfortunately, their behaviors are so obnoxious that those around them repeatedly react by trying to

put them down or criticize them, ultimately making them feel dismissed and inferior.

Possible Solutions for Those Who Deal with Narcissistic Personalities

- Avoid at all costs the desire to criticize them; they are extremely sensitive to it and will attack you back.

- Be honest in what you say and try to compliment them on their strengths, rather than focus on their vulnerabilities.

- Tactfully and indirectly use positivity to change their difficult behaviors.

- Gently try getting them in some type of treatment to change their behaviors if they are aware of their disorder and open to getting help.

- Keep the relationship with them at arm's length and be careful with intimacy.

3. Individuals with **Histrionic Personality Disorder** are driven by an unconscious fear of being ignored. However, their demands for attention make them so difficult and irritating that most people repeatedly try to get away from them and ignore them.

Possible Solutions for Those Who Deal with Histrionic Personalities

- Avoid lengthy and nonessential discussions, and stay focused on the most important issue.

- Don't try to change them or point out to them that their responses are extreme.

- Stay focused on practical and pragmatic ways of solving specific problems with them.

- Don't try to protect them or other people around them from life's realities.

4. Individuals with **Antisocial Personality Disorder** are driven by a fear of being controlled or dominated. This fear makes them over-react by trying to dominate others through manipulation, lies, and even violence, usually without remorse.

Possible Solutions for Those Who Deal with Antisocial Personalities

- Remain skeptical when certain individuals tell you some-body else is bad or evil in some way.

- Remain alert to exaggerated or unusual stories that you are expected to do something about.

- Recognize that these people have aggressive energy, take a lot of risk, and disregard others' rights.

- Pay attention to your gut feelings—these personalities are clever and may try to deceive you.

- Always remind yourself to maintain a healthy skepticism in dealing with these types of personalities.

Again, it is important to recognize that people with these types of personality disorders most often do not recognize their own negative behaviors. Usually, they are not even aware that they need psychological help, and those who are forced to seek help are very resistant and quite difficult to treat effectively. People with antiso-cial personality disorders can be very dangerous due to their lack of a conscience.

27. The Problem: Accepting Bipolar Disorder and Its Treatments

Bipolar disorder, a mood disorder, is a disruptive mental illness that can be spotted during the early teens, although it usually emerges during the early twenties. Combining the bipolar I and bipolar II disorders, which affect men and women equally, bipolar disorder affects a small percent of the population. People with this disorder are highly likely to have recurrent cycles of depressive and manic symptoms and behaviors, which are usually observable by others. Although people with bipolar disorder can be very creative and socially effective, they are prone to function at a lower level of their capabilities due to their illness. Bipolar disorders are quite debilitating, and most of those who suffer from them have recurrences of mania or depression over their lifetimes. Stress factors, including those within the family, may elicit bipolar episodes as well.

Possible Solutions

- Accept and be responsible with the use of psychopharmacological medications.

- Educate yourself about the symptoms, the consequences of leaving the illness untreated, and the best treatments available.

- Recognize the early signs of the manic or depressive cycle, and take action as soon as possible.

- Realize that you will need the services of both a psychologist and a psychiatrist on a regular basis to keep the disorder under control.

- Don't reject psychotropic medications thinking that you can manage your mood swings without them. This seldom if ever works.

- Accept your doctors' recommendations, and don't ignore the concerns of your friends and family. Those around you will see the changes before you can.

PART II

The Family: From the Family
of Origin to the Extended Family

chapter three

FAMILIES

"Home is the place where, when you have to go there,
they have to take you in."

— Robert Frost

A Few Thoughts on the Subject of Families

The family is the most powerful and influential system affecting every individual's life, from the beginning of life to death. The family dictates the values that we ultimately practice as adults, as well as influencing our views and attitudes about friendships, marriage, work, and even politics. We often battle one another as family members, but we cannot comfortably live without each other for very long. We pretend to be separate and independent of our family; we may not even speak to other family members for months at a time. However, instinctually, we long for and seek one another out during a crisis or celebration. No matter how long we have been away from home, most often, within minutes of being there, we feel a sense of peacefulness and familiarity that comforts our soul to the core. So often, we say so much among family members without ever speaking a word. There is an instinctive understanding among one another about everyone's mood or struggles, without the need for explanations and details. Yes, the power that a family has over all of us as individuals is all-encompassing.

I believe that ultimately every system, whether it be a town, a state, or a country, functions similarly to a family. One can argue that some of the systems may function poorly, or are totally dysfunc-tional (like many families), but we cannot live comfortably without them. In our hearts, whether of miles away or around the corner, we view our family as our home. Often, we use the words "family" and "home" interchangeably, and whenever we talk about one or the other, we are totally understood by everyone, with no details or a second thought needed.

There are concerns that the traditional family system is becom-ing a thing of the past, being replaced by a steady stream of activities by parents and children alike involving hobbies, sports, the seeking of hedonistic pleasures, or long hours at work. There is a fast-paced frenzy to everyone's life, which often interferes with the ability to effectively connect and communicate with each other on a regular basis. Besides the fast-paced quality of life today, there are other influences affecting the ability to communicate within and outside the family system. The media and all the technology available today tend to create a selfimposed isolation among family members, each retreating into their rooms pursuing interests on the Internet and social media.

Yes, there are major changes taking place in today's family sys-tem, and it is difficult to predict whether these changes will have a significant negative or positive impact in the future. The outcome remains to be seen.

28. The Problem: Knowing the Importance of Family

I believe that the family is the most important and influential system of our lives. I also believe that maintaining a healthy family system rewards us with a long list of benefits to our quality of life. Finally, I believe that the health and function of the family, like any system, will ultimately be based on the quality of its leadership. Thus, the health of any family system is ultimately dictated by the parents.

Family systems can be divided into three different categories: the family of origin, the nuclear family, and the extended family. Each of these categories can pose wonderful opportunities and benefits to individual members of the family.

It is my opinion that the importance of the family, in general, has diminished over the past twenty-five years, and this is evident in many different ways. I am not necessarily suggesting that these changes are either good or bad, but I believe that many of the traditions of the past have been lost over time. Perhaps it may be best for families today to continue to practice some of the traditional activities and values connected to previous generations, while carefully assessing the impact of the new changes currently being introduced in our lives.

29. The Problem: Knowing Where We Come From, the Family of Origin

Since so much of our personalities come from our parents' genes, our identities are largely based on where we come from, the place we connect with best, and where we naturally feel most comfortable and accepted. For many generations, members of the family of origin—the family into which one is born or adopted—lived under one roof, or in close proximity to one another. Weekend gatherings over at Grandma's house were typical—everyone was expected, and eagerly wanted, to attend. Most often, the gatherings took place around the dinner table, where discussions about everybody's lives, problems, and successes were discussed and shared. These activities maintained a continuity of family life and provided a comforting sense of belonging that offered everyone a warm feeling of togetherness. Sometimes, family members felt trapped or unable to move away and create their own lives, separately from the rest of the family, but usually there was a strong desire to connect with the family of origin.

Sadly, during the past twenty-five years, the typical family traditions have changed significantly; parents and siblings move on and are spread across the country, and sometimes even across the world. Additionally, the roles of those who remain in close proximity to one another have also changed significantly. Everyone experiences some losses due to these changes.

The following suggestions may help you gain the benefits of a close family of origin.

Possible Solutions

- Try to spend time with your parents and siblings around the dinner table nightly.

- Discuss the history of the family, especially with children, so they can feel a sense of belonging.

- Utilize relationships with your parents and siblings as a source of help and support.

- Encourage the parents to share their individual histories, listening carefully.

- Take advantage of your family members' experiences and wisdom to improve your quality of life.

- Participate and rejoice in your family members' accomplishments and successes with pride.

- Develop close friendships with your siblings and their spouses and socialize together often.

- Take the time and make the effort to have your children develop close relationships with cousins.

- Don't allow "pride" or "hurt feelings" to disrupt relationships and end communication.

- Don't ignore or remain uninvolved when a family member is struggling and needs your help.

- Create family rituals that will allow everyone to get together as often as possible.

- Acknowledge and respect the leadership in the family system, and utilize their wisdom well.

- Mourn together, cry together, share together, and rejoice in each other's happy successes.

- Never allow feelings of jealousy to enter your thoughts, feelings, or behavior in families.

- Always offer your help to any family member in need; you will most likely get it back.

30. The Problem: Managing the Nuclear Family

The structure and activities of the nuclear family have perhaps gone through the greatest evolution of the past twenty-five years. The traditional roles of the leaders of the nuclear family have changed; while in the long past mothers typically stayed at home, today they're more likely to work full-time. While many of the responsibilities at home are still managed by the women, men are much more actively involved in carrying out some of these duties. Children's lives have become more difficult and complicated. Children are no longer allowed to play and grow up slowly until they develop the necessary skills and maturity. After-school activities have become much more common and time-intensive, and there is always a struggle to accomplish them all. Traditional nightly dinners around the table have often been replaced by everyone eating when they can or when they want, and usually eating whatever they want. There seems to be a rush to do it all by every family member, a national movement to have every child involved in multiple sports activities, and sometimes one or both parents traveling on many weekends to different parts of the country so that their children can compete in tournaments. Competition and success seem to be the driving forces imposed on children from as young as four all the way into college. Unfortunately, at times, homework ends up being "squeezed in" between all the other activities. Also, the line between parents and children has become blurred. Children feel free to speak their minds and express their thoughts and feelings, regardless of how socially inappropriate those behaviors might be; often, parents model those same behaviors.

Yes, the nuclear family has changed drastically, but some of its more valued activities can still remain intact. The following suggestions are offered in the hope of helping you create a healthier and better balance in your nuclear family.

Possible Solutions

- Try hard to have as many family dinners together as possible every week.

- Use the family room to hang out as a whole family, rather than all retreating to their rooms.

- Put aside at least one day a week for children to just sit around and play, talk, and do nothing.

- Before you plan anything else, make sure to set up a daily homework schedule for your child.

- Be very clear with your children what your expectations are, and be sure that they are carried out.

- Demand that everyone in the family take care of and put away their personal belongings.

- Create family rituals and traditions to celebrate holidays, birthdays, and other special occasions.

- Make sure that you consider time with the family when choosing careers and job opportunities.

- Try to maintain order and consistency in the family so that everyone understands the expectations.

- Set up a "family day" on a weekly basis so everyone knows not to schedule anything else that day.

- Make time to catch up with what went on in everyone's life daily before going to sleep.

- Call or get in touch often with family members who are not liv-ing in the home.

31. The Problem: The Extended Family, the Sources of Our History

Families, the source of who we are, the source that we connect best with, the source that we need the most, the system that we turn to when no one else is there, must be maintained to survive. Maintaining a family history and passing it on from generation to generation is a gift that we often waste. In the past, people were able to name and talk about the third cousin, second removed, on the grandmother's side of the family and where they live now. Now, first cousins often don't stay in contact or even know one another. The celebration of family traditions is usually carried out with only immediate family and friends, rather than the extended family. Valuable traditions that often were carried out from one generation to another are now lost by the time the second generation takes over. The ethnic backgrounds of families were often a source of pride and honor, unlike today, when many people don't have a clear sense of their ethnicity. The loss of connections with the extended family system is also a loss of valuable resources that can be utilized to benefit all the family's members. Finally, the gene pool information that the extended family can offer is also lost, and the ability to know the physical and mental histories of past family members (which can help to better understand and select appropriate treatments) are also lost.

Sadly, today there is a clear disconnection from family history. The following suggestions may be useful to those of you who want the benefits of the extended family system.

Possible Solutions

- Make sure to keep in touch with uncles, aunts, cousins, and other distant relatives.
- Whenever you gather with these family members, ask questions and discuss family history.
- Invite extended family members whenever you are celebrating important events in your life.
- Invite elderly members of the family to your home for an afternoon of eating and socializing.
- Try to plan "cousins' get-together parties" and make sure that their children are also included.
- Whenever a member of the extended family is in crisis, always reach out and offer your help.
- When you need to, reach out to extended family members and share your burden with them.
- Try to have all-encompassing, formal, extended family gatherings that include everyone.
- When you are aware of a family member seeking a job or in need of a service, help the best that you can.
- Create a detailed, inclusive family tree and share it with everyone.

chapter four

PARENTING CHILDREN

"It is easier to build strong children than to repair broken men."

— Frederick Douglass

A Few Thoughts on the Subject of Parenting

Parenting is being given detailed and focused attention here because it is an extremely difficult job and the results have life-changing and at times tragic consequences for both those who parent and those who are being parented. I have broken the subject down into different stages in order to offer suggestions for the specific difficulties faced at different stages of a child's development.

I have also included the subject of "parenting the parent" because, very often, parents age and are unable to effectively manage life's responsibilities and care for themselves. The job of parenting—for infants and children, adolescents, young adults, married adults, and finally, parents themselves—is one of the most difficult, life-encompassing occupations possible, one in which success is defined purely on the basis of being able to say, "I have parented, I have made it through, and I have survived!"

I want to say that "good parenting" doesn't really exist, because our ability to carry out this responsibility is strongly influenced by many other factors, some of them healthy and some of them unhealthy. We are influenced by: what we saw our parents do, developing our own biases as to what we should do, what other parents do, the situation we face at the moment, the mood that we may be in, what ethnic background we come from, what circumstances we are faced with at the moment, and the personality of the child, just to list a few factors.

As a disclaimer, what I offer now are only some guidelines that you may want to consider and can generally be applied in most common circumstances for most children in your parenting journey. I do not offer you guarantees that these interventions will work all the time, or even some of the time. They may work with one child, but not another. They may work one day, but not the next day. Some professionals are convinced that they have the right methods and guidelines to help raise healthy children and there are even parents who have convinced themselves that they have done an ideal job. I struggle when I try to accept these positions.

32. The Problem: Teaching Infants and Children

As parents, we have the awesome responsibility to know many things so that we can teach children anything and everything we can. We know that if we do a fair job, they can grow and function effectively in the world with family, friends, co-workers, partners, and themselves. There are so many things we can do, say, model, and express that can help develop an infant into a fun child, a responsible adolescent, and a well-balanced and satisfied adult. The following are some examples of some things to know, remember, and carry out when we deal with infants and children.

Possible Solutions

- When your baby laughs and you do the same, you're teaching it to socialize with others.

- One-year-old infants who are allowed to take the lead during their struggles are more persistent at solving tasks.

- For children, play is their occupation. It makes them grow emotionally, socially, and intellectually.

- Babies listen and learn right from birth as they respond to words and tone of voice.

- Babies need routines and schedules to know when they eat, when they nap, and when they play.

- Autonomy is the need to be independent, free to act and think for oneself, so allow the child to find their way.

- Children learn values like honesty and kindness, and develop morals based on what they see.

- Teach a child the prayer of "thanks" for family, health, and daily bread; they will learn gratitude.

- Children up to thirty-six months of age can't verbalize intense emotions, temper tantrums, or answers to questions.

- Accept the presence of fear in a child up to two years old; it is a natural stage of their development.

- A child playing with toys learns best when a parent encourages and participates in the play.

- Don't force toddlers to share their favorite toys; they have the right to a sense of ownership.

- Don't expect friendships, peer relationships, and cooperative play with other children to develop until thirty months of age.

- When a very young child makes small decisions, they will be at an advantage when they need to make decisions in the future.

- Using physical punishment with a child teaches the child that physical violence is acceptable.

- Teach a child manners and self-control lovingly and with lots of patience and repetition.

- A child gains understanding and control of emotions when you attach words to feelings.

- Preschoolers don't progress at the same pace, and achievements don't equal superior intelligence.

- Imaginative play in preschoolers leads to better concentration on tasks. Don't discourage it.

- The foundation on which intelligence grows is the development of language skills, ages three to six.

- The groundwork to make and sustain friendships is laid early, supported and supervised by parents.

- A child who does not have a close relationship with its parents is vulnerable to negative peer pressure.

- A child explores a sense of self through pretend play roles, in which they try out other identities.

- The core of self-confidence and autonomy in a child develops through mastering activities.

- Chores are not be assigned to a child as punishment, but instead presented as helping others.

- Giving your children a daily chore will build a sense of responsibility and achievement.

- School-age children are fearful of making mistakes and looking foolish in the eyes of others.

- During childhood, the most important skills to master for success are reading and writing.

- Children who are unpopular are most likely to have deficits and limitations in social skills.

- Rituals, routines, and traditions provide a sense of love, security, and stability for both children and parents.

- School-age children have intense concerns about what others think and where they fit socially.

- School-age children struggle between autonomy and fear of straying too far from family security.

- Monitor school-age children's amount of time spent daily on TV, phone, and computer games.

- Remember, family is the most influential factor in a child's moral and social development.

- Physiological changes allow children from the ages of six to eight to begin to draw moral distinctions from within.

- Children need to assert their independence by testing limits; be sure to set and enforce them.

- When you chart progress of a child's manners, don't make a scene; you will be engaging in rude behaviors.

- Examples of politeness and good manners must be given to a child with detailed instructions.

33. The Problem: Parenting Infants and Young Children

To thoroughly address this subject would require a book in itself. Here, I offer only some minimal information and general guidelines, so that parents can have a general understanding of some of the activities needed for normal childhood development.

The first six years of a child's life are the most crucial in building social, emotional, interpersonal, and thinking skills. When parenting infants and young children, it is important to realize that the first six years will ultimately influence how well the individual functions as an adult. I think that, ideally, one of the parents should be the full-time, primary caretaker for this stage of the child's development, in order to provide the child with the required consistency, love, attention, stimulation, and multitude of experiences that a child needs. The child's needs change over the course of different stages of development, and knowing what is most important that a parent can teach and do is probably one of the more significant responsibilities of a primary caretaker. Again, the most important areas to focus on in the child's development include social, emotional, interpersonal, behavioral, and thinking skills.

The following are some suggestions that can be utilized during a child's first stages of development.

Possible Solutions

- Teach your infant to trust you; respond with love and sensitivity to cries of pain.

- Teach your infant to feel safe; give lots of physical contact; play, smile, hug, and talk a lot.

- Teach your infant to manage fear; respect, acknowledge, and accept the fears. Give it some time.

- Teach your child problem solving; let a child watch, try on its own, struggle, and repeat.

- Teach your child social skills; spend time with other babies, and invite babies and parents to play dates.

- Teach your child structure; create rituals and routines for eating, sleeping, playing, and downtime.

- Teach your child independence; let your baby self-soothe, cry himself to sleep, and be separate.

- Teach your child values; teach the meaning of love and respect.

- Teach the child self-control; say no, but do not yell or spank. Do not use long explanations to discipline.

- Teach your child language; read, talk, ask open-ended questions, label things, and play games.

- Teach your child self-acceptance; it is okay if they are different.

- Teach your child to value the self: physical attributes, possessions, special skills, and passions.

- Teach your child responsibility: homework, chores, commitments, promises, and life skills.

- Teach your child the importance of education; hard work, reading, experimentation, and open questions.

- Teach your child safety; play the "what if" game, teach them about dangerous actions

- Teach your child reasonableness in thoughts, behaviors, emotions, values, and self-control.

- Teach your child discipline: consequences, rewards and punishment, and responsibility.

34. The Problem: On Being an Effective Parent

Common knowledge tells us the definition of a parent: to act as a mother or father to someone. Simple enough! The Oxford Dictionary's definition of "the proper role of a parent" offers a more comprehensive explanation and set of responsibilities. It states, "The proper role of a parent is to provide encouragement, support, and access to activities that enable the child to master key developmental tasks. The parent is their child's first teacher, and should remain their best teacher throughout life." This definition is dear, but not necessarily simple. However, my view of being a parent is that it is ultimately the most difficult, all-encompassing job in one's life. The process often feels like going on a journey with a broken-down car, with no directions or map, not really knowing where you're going, and in the end, finding out that you never really got where you thought you should have been anyway. So you have the simple defi-nition of a parent, the more complicated definition of the "proper" role of a parent, and my personal observations of what the job of trying to be a proper parent really feels like.

I want to pass on some lessons that I have learned about healthy parenting from my personal life, my professional life, and my observations of other people. The following general suggestions apply to parenting children ranging in ages from six to sixty.

Possible Solutions

- Know that a child must always feel loved, from your words, actions, and deeds.

- Know that children have different needs and stages, but always need structure and discipline.

- Know that a correct definition of "discipline" is "to teach," rather than to criticize, belittle, and punish.

- Know that a child must know that you are in control and capable of mastering yourself.

- Know that a child must learn to self-soothe and manage the extremes of their emotions.

- Know that your main job is to raise a self-sufficient, independent, and well-functioning adult.

- Know that your child learns best from what they see you do, rather than what you have to say.

- Know that your children should be respected, seen, and treated as the unique individuals they are.

- Know that a child practices the "divide and conquer" game with you and your partner.

- Don't ask your child to be involved, or take sides, in your relationship with your partner.

- Don't ever allow your child to challenge or question your decisions and judgment.

- Never decide or take action based only on strong feelings or impulsive behaviors.

- Don't convince yourself that you are responsible for your child's happiness.

- Believe that it is okay if, at times, you don't know what to do as a parent. Seek useful help.

- Remember to accept the child you have, rather than wish for the perfect child you have fantasized about.

- Identify your child's strengths and talents, and help fully develop them.

- Never openly compare your child with your other children or with someone else's children.

- Don't offer your child solutions until they have tried everything to find their own solutions.

- Remember that whenever you rescue a capable child, you are implying that they are not capable of rescuing themselves.

- Don't tell your child that they are great and brilliant at everything. They will not handle failures.

- Don't make rules that are unreasonable; you will fail both you and your child in the end.

- Structure is crucial in raising a child, so remember, "If you fail to plan, you plan to fail."

- Never make threats to your child that you are not prepared to carry out; say it and mean it.

- Remember, you don't have to address a problem with your child immediately. Think first!

35. The Problem: Parenting Teenagers

It has been said, "Raising teenagers is like nailing Jello to a tree." First of all, it is important to recognize that being a teenager is quite difficult, especially in today's complex world of technology. Teenagers struggle with developing an identity while their sense of self is in transition. They struggle with finding a place in their social system where they feel accepted and comfortable. Additionally, they are bombarded by information like never before, and they struggle with trying to understand, process, and incorporate it in their lives. They further struggle with the temptations of drugs, alcohol, sexual impulses, and competition with peers. Finally, they struggle with physiological changes, flooding of hormones, and their efforts to become a responsible adult. No, being a teenager today is definitely not easy, and their emotional volatility makes them more difficult to parent without creating conflicts—or, worse yet, disconnection.

The following suggestions are offered to parents who deal specifically with teenagers.

Possible Solutions

- First of all, whenever you are dealing with a teenager, don't overreact to their overreaction.

- By the time your teen is thirteen years old, you must pass the homework responsibility on to them.

- After discussion, allow your seventeen-year-old to choose their college of choice.

- After allowing an exchange of opinions, you still have the right to say, "Because I said so."

- Know that teens must rebel against the rules to develop their own philosophies; it's normal.

- Know that there is a very fine line between offering guidance and running your teen's life.

- Know that teens want parents to understand, appreciate, and love them while they struggle.

- It's important to keep the channels of communication open in both good and bad times.

- Allow your teenager to have their own goals, and ensure that they keep their standards high.

- Teach your teen the importance of trust, and how to repair it when they damage it.

- Be most available between 3:00 to 7:00 pm, since that's when teens get into the most trouble because those are the times that they are out of school and unsupervised.

- When talking to a teen, be respectful, keep clear rules, and share expectations, but do it all gently.

- Whatever you say or do when dealing with a teen, remember to keep a sense of humor.

- Teach teens self-care, the value of one's word, respect for oneself and others, and responsibility.

- Talk about healthy and unhealthy use of electronics; check on what websites they're visiting.

- Things that are important to focus on when observing, listening, or discussing:

  - Let them know that you are proud of who they are and what they do.

  - Listen to their hopes, fears, confusions, and dreams for their future.

  - Ask questions about school, what subjects they struggle with, and what help they may need.

  - Help them think about and teach them about time management and space organization.

  - Have frank and open talks about alcohol, drugs, the law, health, and money.

- Have a serious and open discussion about sex, safety, consent, and violation of others' rights.

- Talk, talk, and talk to your teenager, but even more important, listen carefully.

36. The Problem: Addressing Sexuality with Children

Many parents are uncomfortable discussing sex with their children, and often the subject is totally ignored. I think that children should be educated about what is healthy and unhealthy about sex, what is appropriate or inappropriate, and how to develop a healthy attitude about sexuality. I suggest that, first and foremost, parents should review their own discomfort and biases about the subject of sex so that they do not pass them on to their child. Discussing or sharing the wrong information, including suggestions that sexual activities are somehow bad, can cause significant difficulties for the child in their future. I think that, at the minimum, children should have the opportunity to ask all the questions they want, learn some basic information, and acquire some general knowledge about the natural and normal urges and activities of sexuality.

The following are some simple guidelines to consider when addressing sexuality with your child.

Possible Solutions

- If you do not know what to say to open the discussion, learn from books, the Internet, or your pediatrician.

- Always respond to your child's questions about sex and sexuality simply, openly, and honestly.

- Don't make things up or give strange names to sexual organs; correctly label what they are.

- Keep the sharing of information on sexuality at the appropriate level for the child's age.

- Discuss the subject of sexuality as something that is normal, pleasurable, and appropriate.

- Make clear under what circumstances sex might be appropriate.

- Always share what to do when your child feels touched inappropriately, uncomfortable, or threatened.

- Encourage children of all ages never to listen to anyone who tells them to keep secrets about sex acts being shown or done to them.

- Discuss, especially with teens, coercive behaviors, respecting "no means no," consent, and love.

- Be open and encourage questions on sexuality from your children, regardless of age.

chapter five

PARENTING YOUNG ADULT CHILDREN AND YOUR OWN AGING PARENTS

"Everything can be taken from a man but one thing—the last of the human freedoms—to choose one's attitude in any given set of circumstances, to choose one's own way."

— Viktor Frankl

A Few Thoughts on Parenting Adult Children

A woman named Ruth Sanford wrote a one-page story, "Loving with An Open Hand," designed to cleverly address the problem of how we as parents, with all of our loving intentions, can cripple our children, especially young adults. Her story goes like this: "A compassionate person, seeing a butterfly struggle to free itself from its cocoon, and wanting to help, very gently loosened the filaments to form an opening. The butterfly was freed, emerged from the cocoon, fluttered about and could not fly. What your compassionate person did not know was that only through the birth struggle can the wings grow strong enough for flight. Its shortened life will be spent on the ground, it never knew freedom, never really lived."

Later in the story she said, "I am learning that I must free the one I love, for if I clutch or cling, try to control, I lose what I try to hold." She finished the one-page story with the following: "I love you so much that I can set you free to walk beside me in joy and in sadness…I cannot always keep my hands off the cocoon, but I am getting better at it!"

I love this story because it addresses a national trend: the help provided to adult children by parents. Although such help is given purely out of love, it ultimately cripples one's ability to grow up and take responsibility for oneself.

I believe that through struggling and suffering as necessary, we gain strength and grow. Over recent years, adult children have been allowed to depend on their parents financially and emotionally, way past the acceptable age. Many adult children remain totally dependent into the late twenties and thirties before they choose to take responsibility for themselves. It is difficult to decipher whether the parents are allowing it to happen, or whether the adult children strongly resist the responsibilities of a grownup.

Many parents feel trapped by their children's demands, often convinced that they are bad parents. There are many variations on this theme, but usually the results keep the parents totally responsible for their child's well-being while keeping them from maturing, growing up, and moving on. Unfortunately, this cycle can create some psychological difficulties for the parents, the adult child, and the family.

37. The Problem: Developing Unhealthy Patterns

It is difficult, most of the time, to clearly assess the main source of your difficulties and who the main contributor to your problems are. It is difficult to conclude whether adult children develop unhealthy patterns of dependency due to their parents' willingness to accept their immaturity, or whether these patterns stem from resistance to the discomfort of accepting the responsibilities that come with adulthood. As a clinician, I can recognize certain unhealthy patterns that seem to be created early in the development of interdependency between parent and child. These patterns are very difficult to address when both parents are trapped in a cycle and the adult child views the pattern as normal and comfortable to live with. I believe that it is useful to provide some examples of the unhealthy patterns that develop through the cycle of codependency between parent and child. I hope that parents or adult children see themselves in these examples and try to make changes.

A. **The typical adult children in a codependency cycle tend to present one of the following problems. They:**

- Are forever sad, gloomy, and miserable in their ways, and need to be cheered on and rescued. They are convinced, and convince their parents, that their general unhappiness is their parents' responsibility.

- Are forever in crises, or constantly create chaos in their lives, and the parents are forever rescuing them, trying hard to straighten them out so that they can become self-sufficient.

- Have unreasonable expectations of their parents, and have made them the cook, the maid, and their personal financial institution. They are very harsh in their criticism when the parents fail to deliver, and angrily express their disappointment.

- Have a sense of entitlement that their needs should be fully satisfied, while they are comfortably floundering through life searching for the perfect school, the perfect job, and a perfect lifestyle. They demand to be taken care of until they find themselves.

- Profess incompetence in their ability to do, think, decide, and commit to any decision or responsibility. These problems leave the parents to do the worrying, the thinking, and the necessary legwork for them until the child has figured it out.

- Forever promise to go on their own; sometimes they actually do for a short period of time, but quickly they come back home, usually broke and asking for more care and support. The request for support quickly turns into demands, combined with guilt trips. The time they spend at home turns into months and even years of dependency.

- Have the arrogance to be critical of their parents, to blame them for their misery, and attack them verbally and even physically when they don't get their way. The parents usually take the blame and assume responsibility for their needs and unhappiness.

B. **Why did these adult children refuse to grow up? Possible reasons:**

- They did not get the love that they needed and wanted, so they are very angry and want to punish their parents. They may or may not be conscious of both the lack of love and the anger.

- They are forever stuck in the role of a child who has to be cared for, and they see the parents only in the role of caretakers. They typically have a difficult time viewing themselves as adults.

- They are very afraid of being independent and self-sufficient, because they view independence as loneliness, requiring disconnection from the family.

- They get caught up with perfectionism, so they are frightened of failing or making a mistake. They prefer the comfort of home and give the responsibility to their parents. Ultimately, the fear of being responsible is so overwhelming that they decide not to grow up. Of course, we cannot rule out those who are lazy, narcissistic, or just spoiled.

Possible Solutions

- Demand to be treated with respect; never accept verbal or physical threats or abuse.

- Give yourself the right to say "no" to any demand to take care of their needs.

- Take responsibility for some mistakes you have made and let go of the guilt forever.

- Give yourself the right to give up responsibility for your adult child once and for all.

- Engage in healthy parenting by offering your adult child appropriate guidance. Remind them that you love who they are, and you have total faith that they will succeed on their own without your help.

- Re-evaluate your parenting style and recognize if you were or are:

  - Too strict, not allowing your child to feel worthy and self-confident on their own.

  - Too lenient, suggesting you do not care, are too insecure to stand your ground, and set no structure.

- Too anxious, too afraid to let your child grow to deal with the unknown and the dangers they will face.

- Be totally honest with your child about your mistakes and poor parenting, and:
  - Openly and honestly acknowledge your shortcomings and failures, and apologize to him or her.
  - Make a list of all the right and wrong things you may have done; you are not perfect.
  - Once you have completed these lists and assessed your parenting, forgive yourself.

- Now make sure to carry out the role of a healthy parent by teaching your child:
  - How to effectively care for their physical, mental, financial, and overall well-being.
  - How to make a living so that they can completely care for their own needs.
  - How to be proud and develop their desire to be compe-tent and self-sufficient.
  - The importance of give-and-take when dealing with others in their lives.

- Most important, let your adult child know that you love and respect them so much that, from now on, you'll allow them to live their lives without interference, and allow them to fail if they must so that they will learn how they can get up and grow through hardship.

38. The Problem: Parenting Grown-up Children

In the eyes of a parent, a child remains a child whether they are six, sixteen, or sixty. Unfortunately, sometimes married, adult children want to remain children and never really emotionally leave home and grow up, remaining dependent on their parents for child care, financial and emotional support, and decision making. At the same time, many of these married children view themselves as mature grownups. Today, many married people in their forties expect, at times even demand, that their parents take care of many of their responsibilities. Many children today are being raised by grandparents, and many young adults expect their parents to provide some or most of the down payment required when they buy their first house. Others expect their parents to financially contribute to their quality of life. Married people, ranging in age from the early thirties to late forties, may believe that they should have all the luxuries, amenities, and freedoms that their parents did; otherwise, they think that their lives are burdened with unnecessary sacrifices.

There is no question that some of these problems have been created and maintained by the parents of this generation, who believed that it was their responsibility to ensure that their children had everything and were happy. If you consider yourself to be a mature adult between the ages of thirty to fifty, it is useful to consider whether you practice the following behaviors, and whether you and your parents have an unhealthy co-dependent relationship.

Possible Solutions

- At your age, you are not entitled to everything you desire just because others, or your parents, have it.

- If you have children, the responsibility to raise them is yours, not your family's.

- It is irrational to think at your age that your quality of life should be the same as your parents.

- Old enough to get married? Then be old enough to emotionally divorce from your family of origin by eliminating the co-depentncy.

- When married, make sure you develop a mutual philosophy by combining your beliefs with your mate's.

- Never go to your family members or parents and complain in any way about your partner.

- Make a deal with your partner to defend each other's family members, not criticize them; this will set you free to share without feeling disloyal to your family.

- Set clear boundaries between your parents and family about what is and is not their business.

- Buy a house, a condo, a car, and even a cell phone when you, not your parents, can afford it.

- Remember that you must forgive your parents for not being perfect; they did their best.

- If you don't like your parents for who they are, you still have to respect them for the roles they play.

- Respect and honor your parents and family as you want your children one day to do for you.

39. The Problem: Parenting the Parents

Today's elderly parents live much longer and often, at a certain age, their ability to manage their health, finances, transportation, and even daily living requirements diminishes significantly enough to require additional help. There is an Italian word, "rimbambito," which loosely translates into, "re-entering the childlike stage; the inability to function independently due to old age." At this stage of development, the child may be forced to take on the role of parenting the parents. This is a difficult stage for everyone, because the parents typically do not want to give up their independence in decision making and are in denial about their faltering abilities. The child, on the other hand, does not want the responsibility, and often the struggle, of convincing the parents to give up certain activities, nor of making difficult decisions for them. At times, against their wishes, these responsibilities are imposed on one child in the family. Anger and resentment often develop between siblings when debating who should be responsible for what when managing the elderly parents.

The following are some examples of problems that an adult child may be faced with in dealing with elderly parents who can no longer effectively manage their daily care and other important responsibilities in their lives, and Possible Solutions to these problems.

Problems and Possible Solutions

1. The problem: The parent demands that their needs be taken care of completely and immediately.

Solution: It is very important to establish a set of rules on how you choose to help your elderly parents. As honestly and fairly as you can, decide what you are willing and able to do so that you will satisfy some of their needs without sacrificing yourself or acquiescing to control. When you have made the list of responsibilities, you need to be very clear in relaying them to the elderly parent, letting them know what you can and cannot do, and when and how you can do it. It is crucial that you follow your list and be fully responsible, to the best of your ability, in keeping it under your own control. You have to make your responsibilities a "want to," not a "have to," when making your list.

2. The problem: The parent requires an aide to manage their daily life needs due to a reduction in life skills, but refuses and claims not to need one.

Solution: This is quite typical of an elderly parent, who refuses to accept their limitations and give up their independence. As the responsible decision maker, the adult child has to decide whether the parent truly needs help, try to respect the parent's position as best as possible, and when it is totally necessary, state clearly to the elderly parent, "I'm sorry that you are unable or unwilling to accept that you need help. I love you, I'm responsible for you, and I have to do what I think is best for you, even when it is upsetting and diminishing your freedom to decide. I am making the decision for you, and that's what will have to happen."

3. The problem: The parent must have 24/7 help in the house, but quickly rejects the idea.

Solution: This problem is almost universal for most elderly parents and their children. The best approach is to present to the parent, in the most loving and gentle way possible, that someone has to be with them for their own safety and well-being. The adult child has to become educated about the options available, including the cost and availability of eldercare centers in the parents' community. If the elderly parents continue to refuse the suggestion, it is best to offer what is called "a forced choice." The adult child has to explain: "You'll either accept help in the house 24/7, or for your safety, I have no choice but to bring you to a nursing home." The forced choice has to be very clear, strongly presented, and final.

4. The problem: The parent refuses to make a will, transfer assets, or accept co-ownership of assets.

Solution: Unfortunately, the child has no real power to enforce those reasonable and necessary expectations. However, making an appointment with an elder-law attorney who can explain the pros and cons of carrying out versus not carrying out these various activities can sometimes convince the parent to make the right choice. Again, it is crucial for the adult child to educate oneself and the parent on the pros and cons of these different subjects.

5. The problem: The parent refuses to take prescribed medication, or takes it only partially.

Solution: While you can never really be sure whether the elderly parent will take medication, the ultimate solution may be for you or a helper to dispense the medication as required. The problem should also be addressed with the parent's family doctor present. Be sure not to be critical of the parent, and show your concerns regarding the problem rather than your frustration when talking to the parent and doctor together.

6. The problem: The parent's driving ability is now dangerous; they refuse to stop driving.

Solution: In some states, there are laws prohibiting elderly people from driving a car if they fail to pass a driving test after a certain age. In other states, there are no laws whatsoever, and the responsibility is often placed on the family doctor or adult children to forbid the elderly individual from driving. Check the laws in your state, and if you are convinced that your elderly parent is endangering people, then it may be your responsibility to take away the keys and/or the car. Try very hard to explain your decision gently and offer Possible Solutions as to how the elderly parent can get around and go places they need to go.

40. The Problem: Dealing with Death

We all know that death is inevitable; no one can escape it. Yet we cannot help but be devastated when someone close to us dies. Somebody defined bereavement, grief, and mourning this way: "Bereavement is the state of having lost a significant other to death. Grief is the personal response to the loss. Mourning is the public expression of the loss." Often people ask if there is such a thing as "normal grief." The answer is yes and no. Grief reactions depend on who we are, who we have lost, our relationship with that person, the circumstances around their passing, and how much the loss affects our day-to-day functioning. I believe that the process of "grieving" is like a person's fingerprints; everyone's is unique. The symptoms of grieving are based on three different experiences, which may vary with time, and include some of the following: emotional (sadness, anxiety, anger, etc.), behavioral (crying, restlessness, pulling away from others, etc.), and physical (fatigue, upset stomach, pain, etc.). The duration of grief also varies depending on the individual. The time required to recover from grief can vary a lot from person to person. The strongest upsetting reactions are around significant dates, holidays, and birthdays. It is important to know that, although children grieve, they do so differently by asking questions out of the blue, or talk about that person months later. Amazingly, we all recover from a loss to some degree; the weird thing about devastating losses is that life goes on. While we may wonder how we could possibly live through such a huge loss, somehow the world keeps turning, the seconds keep on ticking. We somehow survive and go on with life!

Possible Solutions

- Everybody will grieve a death; you cannot go around it and ignore it, you have to go through it.

- Don't hide or make things up with kids; show them your feelings, and simply say what happened.

- Over days, weeks, and months, children will ask questions about the death; be honest and answer.

- While grieving, find supportive people; reach out and share your feelings about the loved one.

- Find a way to memorialize your loved one; contribute to a charity, plant a tree, etc.

- Create a list of funny memories of them, and when you think of the loved one, read it.

- Early in the grief period, postpone major life changes, take care of your health, and keep a journal.

- Be prepared that people want you to move on with life; it is up to you when and how.

- Try to understand that different people mourn differently; don't think that others don't care.

- It is crucial that you keep your daily routines, and engage fully in living life as best you can.

- Consider joining a grief-support group with people who have suffered a similar loss.

- If you find yourself unable to cope for too long, seek a grief counselor for additional help.

PART III

Romantic Relationships:
From Dating to Divorce

chapter six

ROMANTIC RELATIONSHIPS

"All mankind love a lover. The earliest demonstrations
of complacency and kindness are nature's most
winning pictures."

— Ralph Waldo Emerson

A Few Thoughts on Romantic Relationships

Romantic relationships are without a doubt one of the most important factors in our happiness and well-being. But I believe that books,
the media, and other public sources of information often give people
unrealistic expectations of romance. There is no question that the
need to connect and develop a "one-to-one" level of intimacy with
another human being is very powerful, and it drives most unattached
people for most of their waking hours. We are social beings, and our
connection with others often defines our self-worth, how positively
or negatively we perceive ourselves, and even how happy or unhappy
we feel in life. Romantic relationships can generate extreme emotions from joy to misery. We can actually "die of a broken heart" over
the breakup of a romantic relationship.

While love is usually considered the most important factor in
a romantic relationship, I believe that the word is used too often as
the ultimate measure of a relationship's success, when other factors
are more significant in predicting its survival. For example, there

is evidence that building a friendship with a partner is one of the best predictors of a healthy relationship. Some other factors considered important for the survival of a romantic relationship include the abilities to: have a healthy fight, show mutual respect, maintain transparency and honesty, eliminate gridlock in arguments, create a strong sense of trust, remain loyal to each other, and communicate honestly and openly.

Unfortunately, the chances of a permanent relationship surviving are not that high. I believe that people often do not truly take the opportunity to resolve their difficulties and differences. I think that some couples do not accept responsibility for the survival of the relationship, and tend to consider only their level of happiness instead. A permanent relationship is a commitment that should be taken more seriously, less selfishly, and with a greater sense of respect for the institution of marriage.

The selection of a partner also affects a relationship's chance of survival. Honesty and transparency should be practiced at all times during the dating process. Recognize that not all of your needs will be satisfied in any relationship, and be prepared for some disappointments. The illusion that some people engage in—thinking, "I'm not worried; I'm going to change the other person as soon as…"—will not happen. No, we do not have the power to really change people; what you choose is ultimately what you get, so select carefully!

41. The Problem: Finding a Life Partner

The world of dating today is complicated at best and seems to have some irrational rules. There are rules about appearing "too needy," because it will scare prospects off; rules about how long one should wait before calling someone back, etc. It's not surprising that most people are unhappy and confused about today's dating scene, and many people give up trying to date altogether. The most difficult part of the dating situation is that many people looking for a partner do not know where to go to try to meet someone or how to behave when an opportunity does present itself. It's sad to see that so many people feel dejected, isolated, and lonely while trying to navigate the many pitfalls of dating.

What can anyone interested in finding a partner do to have a better chance of meeting their soulmate?

Possible Solutions

- Never, under any circumstances, try to become a chameleon; just "be yourself."

- Ignore all the ridiculous dating rules of today and follow your gut, your own common sense.

- Be direct, say what you want, and analyze whether you and your partner both want the same things.

- Don't ignore signs from someone who is not interested in you; it's time to move on.

- Tell someone directly but gently when you are not interested. Don't just disappear.

- Never make an impulsive decision based on someone's looks. Ultimately, that's not enough.

- Never pressure anyone to give you more than they're willing to give; in the end, you lose it all.

- Don't assume that you will change somebody's mind or personality; that's not possible.

- Don't ask if someone loves you. It is much more significant and true when he or she lets you know or tells you outright.

- Remember we often lie to ourselves when we refuse to accept the reality of the status of the relationship; know when it's over.

- Don't take rejection personally. Not everyone we meet is a match, either for you or them.

- Remember my 25% rule on dating: 25% of the time, you're interested and the other person isn't; 25% of the time, you're not interested and the other person is; 25% of the time, neither of you are interested; and 25% of the time, you're both interested and you have a match!

42. The Problem: Practicing Healthy Dating Rules

So you've found someone, and you start dating them with high hopes and expectations. Many people depend solely on their emotions and gut reactions, and unfortunately put aside common sense and logic in an effort to evaluate whether they have a compatible match. Ideally, selecting a long-term partner requires a series of steps that should be carried out in a certain chronological order.

The following suggestions, usually practiced during the early stages of the relationship, should be seriously considered if you believe you may have found someone special and think that you have a good chance for a long-term future together.

Possible Solutions

- Certainly follow your heart, but never ignore your mind before you make a final decision.

- Know that a healthy and loving bond in a relationship is comprised of a set of multiple dynamics.

- Recognize that patterns influencing long-term relationships are not always evident early on.

- Be sure that you understand each dynamic listed below to your satisfaction before you go to the next stage.

- Pace the speed of your relationship to ensure that you form a strong and loving bond.

- Change is possible, but you need: insight into yourself, new information, motivation, and time. These are the stages:

- "Knowing" requires that you suspend judgment until you get to know the other's gut feelings.

- "Trusting" requires that you observe the other in different settings, situations, and systems of life.

- "Feeling" requires knowing whether the other person meets most of your needs, and you meet theirs.

- "Committing" requires a persevering, unwavering devotion to fulfill what has been promised.

- "Sexual intimacy" requires the understanding that there is no casual sex; sex is always relational.

43. The Problem: Knowing How to Keep a Relationship Alive

You've been dating your partner for a while now, and you are fairly confident that you have met your soulmate. You are convinced that you will love each other forever! Now what? In the long run, love alone will not be enough to make a relationship work. You need to work at your relationship every day to keep it alive and well. I often compare a romantic relationship to a garden: both need ongoing attention and care, otherwise they will die. If you follow the traditional path, you will most likely consider marriage, and it is important not to get lost in the excitement of a wedding and forget to honestly assess both your feelings and your reasoning for your commitment. There are significant factors that play a major role in whether a romantic relationship will ultimately survive.

In order to give yourself and your long-term partner a greater chance at success, you may want to honestly analyze whether your relationship has a majority of the following characteristics.

Possible Solutions

- You and your partner must practice similar values and beliefs.

- You and your partner must create and maintain trust and close friendship with each other.

- You and your partner must have mutual respect for each other, regardless of your differences.

- You and your partner must have similar views on money, child rearing, sex, family, work, and friends.

- You and your partner must be open, and accept each other's influence in decisions.

- You and your partner must be able to have a good fight and still successfully resolve the issue at hand.

- You and your partner must accept that each brings some unsolvable problems to the relationship.

- You and your partner must be open and willing to accept each other's strengths and weaknesses.

- You and your partner must understand that your happiness is your individual responsibility.

- You and your partner must not be critical, defensive, silent, or disrespectful with and to each other.

- You and your partner must be invested in knowing and trying to support each of your most intimate dreams.

- You and your partner must be open, and accept the offers of olive branches for peace.

44. The Problem: Knowing the Commandments of a Loving Relationship

You are now settled in a romantic relationship, and you hope to keep it going successfully. Every system from family, to work, to friendships, to sports, and even to a country has to have certain rules that are followed in order for the system to maintain a healthy order and function well. Unfortunately, there aren't any written rules on how to think, feel, and behave with each other when in a romantic relationship. I would like to offer some important rules that you may want to follow to ensure that your romantic relationship will grow and remain healthy. I'm sure that you can add many more rules to this incomplete list, but I believe that the following commandments should be followed by any couple who wants an ongoing, loving, and healthy relationship.

Possible Solutions

- Recognize that every family shows love differently; your mate's love is not bad, but perhaps just different.

- Never hit your mate below the belt with words or actions, regardless of how hurt and angry you are.

- Decide during a fight whether you want to be right or want to solve the problem; these are clearly different goals.

- Remember that you chose your mate for who they are; don't try to turn them into your clone.

- Practice being a little dumber, blinder, and deafer in conflicts; the results are usually so much better.

- Never make giving your mate a "have to"; always make it a "want to." It shows love most honestly.

- Usually, it's best to give your partner all you have willingly, and you will get back much more in return than you give.

- Remember, there is a big difference between honesty and cruelty.

- Know that if the grass seems much greener on the other side of the fence, the possibility is that your neighbors take better care of it.

- Love your mate for who they are rather than who you wish them to be; no matter what you think, that's who you chose.

- Always maintain a physical relationship and openly discuss your needs, wishes, and desires.

- Don't ignore the problems in your relationship; they don't go away, and most of the time they just grow bigger and more difficult.

45. The Problem: Knowing a Problem-Solving Method

In any relationship, romantic or otherwise, there are always times when two people have very strong and different opinions on a particular issue. Unfortunately, very often we engage in a discussion by talking "at" each other, rather than "to" each other. We don't listen because we are busily preparing to argue our next point, often so involved in presenting our point of view that we do not understand the other person's views, feelings, and logic. Finally, the ultimate damage is done when, because of frustration or hurt, we attack and counterattack each other on a very personal level, totally ignoring the issue at hand. Ultimately, we seldom resolve any particular problem effectively, and we become too frustrated to even acknowledge that we can agree to disagree with each other.

Most issues that most couples face can easily be resolved if they are willing to set aside their pride and listen attentively to each other. I recommend the following technique for couples looking to resolve their difficulties.

Possible Solutions

- Choose only one issue at a time that you want to discuss and resolve; don't argue about everything.

- Make sure that both of you are calm and ready to solve the problem once and for all.

- Have at least half an hour available, no interruptions, to review the various Possible Solutions.

- Select a time period of twenty-five minutes and break it down into five separate five-minute periods.

- Both as a speaker and a listener, always use the word "I" rather than "you" to share your views.

- Use the first five minutes in this way: one of you is the speaker, the other the listener. No interruptions, no discussions.

- Use the next five minutes with the listener summarizing what the speaker said; both need to agree on a summary of the issues.

- Use the next five minutes with the listener becoming the speaker, the speaker becoming the listener, and then following the same rules as above.

- Use the next five minutes with the listener summarizing what the speaker said; both need to agree on the content of the discussion.

- Use the final five minutes with each partner offering as many solutions as possible to solve the problem, and write them down.

- Next, both of you select and try to agree on a solution. If this is not possible, each of you choose the one that you would like to see chosen.

- If you cannot agree on one solution, flip a coin. The winner of the toss chooses the solution he or she likes. The decision is final!

46. The Problem: Dealing with Unsolvable Problems

Most couples, usually after the honeymoon, discover that each partner brings a set of problems to the table that ultimately cannot be solved. Even though we may be convinced that if we had selected a different partner, we would not be faced with these difficulties, both of you will always bring some sort of problem to the table, although the problems may be different with someone else. These problems can cause a lot of pain and are very likely to keep on surfacing over and over without a resolution. At times, if the problems are totally unacceptable, the couple can end up in divorce. Some examples of such problems include differences in: sexual frequency; handling finances; approach to household chores; disciplining children; and drug and alcohol use. The goal in addressing unsolvable problems is to move from a negative gridlock toward a reasonable dialogue.

- Always keep working on and talking about your problems to support and acknowledge the other person's frustration, rather than giving up on each other.

- Listen carefully to your mate's innermost dreams and fears when there is mutual sharing; don't dismiss or belittle them.

- Realize that your partner's overreaction to an unsolvable problem may be due to their past, and most likely painful, history.

- Share with your partner the underlying reasons for your strong emotions on the particular problem being discussed.

- Recognize the underlying reasons for your partner's complaints and overreactions to the problem.

- Don't attack and criticize your partner; share your feelings on the problem without criticism.

- Recognize that many issues are not "right" or "wrong," but simply differences of opinion.

- Don't dismiss your partner's thoughts and feelings; be more understanding.

- Remember that if one of you sees the issue as a problem, it's a problem for both of you and needs to be discussed.

- Explore the symbolic meaning of your individual positions and attitudes on the problem.

- Empathize with your mate's position, and try to accept their feelings on it.

- Negotiate a compromise and show flexibility rather than taking a rigid stand.

47. The Problem: Expressing the Real Thoughts and Feelings

Many difficulties that couples experience are obvious, and they can usually be addressed easily. Other problems tend to be cumulative in nature and can create significant stress on the relationship. Unfortunately, many couples who experience these difficulties tend to react to them with complaints, anger, and criticism rather than trying to resolve or at least talk about them. In a distressed relationship, communication is not really clear, and the underlying issues are seldom if ever expressed openly. Often, couples make all-encompassing complaints and accusations instead. The underlying issues are the most significant and need to be better understood.

The following are some examples of complaints, the possible problems underlying them, and suggested actions to take.

Possible Solutions

1) You say or hear: "I don't know why you never listen. I shouldn't have to nag."

This statement often leads to defensiveness and harsh words between a couple. They have already stopped talking and listening to each other, so one or the other complains.

Instead, try to: be open to your partner's ideas; tell your partner what you need; say what is on your mind more gently; don't be critical and defensive; show more appreciation.

2) You say or hear: "All you ever do is work or talk about work." This statement usually starts a cycle of criticism and defensiveness; neither of your needs are being satisfied, but they have not been expressed directly either.

Instead, try to: express your appreciation and your needs; hear what your partner is longing for, which is usually time with you; recognize possible rejection or abandonment in their past.

3) You say or hear: "Because of all the problems in our lives, we're not close anymore."

This statement addresses the problem of stress, which creates emotional distance and lack of intimacy in a couple. There is a need for emotional intimacy now.

Instead, try to: consider big life changes; take more time for relaxation and bonding; be more honest and vulnerable, and share your deep thoughts and feelings more openly.

4) You say or hear: "You never talk to me anymore."

This statement usually surfaces when the couple is experiencing a general unhappiness and begin to attack and complain about each other rather than communicating the reasons for the unhappiness.

Instead, try to: tell each other what you want rather than complain about what you don't want; listen to what your partner says before you get defensive; try to be a good listener and hear what has been missing in the relationship; recognize that you both have needs, and they must be expressed openly to be satisfied.

5) You say or hear: "All we do is spend time taking care of or talking about the kids now."

This complaint usually hides needs that are not being satisfied, and you or your mate is hiding them behind complaints about the kids.

Instead, try to: discuss your needs more directly and specifically; make your relationship more of a priority; don't complain about the kids; recognize the need for more intimacy.

6) You say or hear: "You can never let things go; you're always having to create drama."

This comment usually involves one being very uncomfortable with an open conflict, and blaming the other when they do not want to discuss the issues.

Instead, try to: recognize that you are avoiding difficult problems; realize that your partner is not willing to bring important problems to the surface; start a gentle discussion, speaking in terms of "I" without criticism or personal attacks; don't attack or defend, just share.

7) You say or hear: "You don't care about what I want or what I think anymore."

This complaint usually suggests that the couple is not interested in each other's needs, dreams, and concerns in general. A disconnection has taken place.

Instead, try to: take turns talking about what each of your needs are; look for ways to compromise in satisfying each other's needs; find ways to champion your partner's dreams and desires; be specific about what you need and want from each other.

8) You say or hear: "What happened to us? There's no more passion, no more fun."

This situation suggests that the couple has not been able to express their angry and negative feelings, and as a result have created an emotional and physical distance from each other.

Instead, try to: recognize what's making you angry and try to express it constructively; truly listen to your partner, find out where the hurt really is, and discuss it openly; talk more openly about difficulties in expressing anger in general.

chapter seven

LOVE, INTIMACY, CONFLICTS, AND CO-DEPENDENCY

"I don't trust people who don't love themselves and tell me, 'I love you.'... There is an African saying which is: Be careful when a naked person offers you a shirt."

— Maya Angelou

48. The Problem: Knowing the Love Languages

According to the author Gary Chapman, certain words and actions that we express toward each other regularly make us feel loved by our partner. He concluded that these words and actions can be broken down into five different love languages in which people express themselves. Supposedly, each of us has a particular love language, and if our desire for this language is not satisfied, we tend to feel empty and disconnected, which often leads to a disinterest in wanting to satisfy our partner's love language. I believe this is a very interesting concept that may help couples find out what it takes for their partner, and for themselves, to feel fully loved in their romantic relationship. Review each of the five love languages described below, and identify yours and your partner's so you can more accurately communicate your love needs, and satisfy your partner's as well.

- **Love Language #1: "Words of Affirmation"**

  Offering verbal compliments and encouraging words to a partner is an expression of love, especially if your partner needs encouragement or feels insecure. A lot of people need words of affirmation to feel loved.

- **Love Language #2: "Quality Time"**

  Giving someone your undivided attention by offering opportunities to talk, going out to eat together, and spending special time together are all expressions of love and acceptance. Some individuals need to be reassured that they are being heard and loved by getting quality time.

- **Love Language #3: "Receiving Gifts"**

  The gift of giving is different for different people. Some people need to have something that can be touched, shown to others, and admired to feel loved. Usually, people who seek "gift giving" as an expression of love may need to be reassured that they are worthy of love; perhaps they may feel insecure about how their parents expressed love to them.

- **Love Language #4: "Acts of Service"**

  The traditional couple tends to have different responsibilities and define them based on a division of labor. Each is responsible for a set of activities while living together and managing the family needs. The expression of love based on "acts of service" refers to when a mate carries out and completes the other person's assigned responsibilities. Those who feel loved by their mate's act of service believe that they are unburdened by their partner.

- **Love Language #5: "Physical Touch"**

  Physical touch is the most recognized method of communicating love to someone. For some people, touch is the best expression of love that they can experience and appreciate.

49. The Problem: Confronting the Difficult Issues

When I treat couples, I tend to mentally categorize what is being communicated by each partner on three different levels: superficial banter, specific complaints, and deeper, underlying issues and needs. I have found that most couples, when seeking my help, want to talk about the last disagreement they had, analyze their partner's flaws, or make all-encompassing, negative statements about their partner. Admittedly, I find myself only half-listening to the bantering and asking myself questions like: What is this really about? What are the real underlying issues that they are not talking about right now?

The three categories into which I mentally put this information are:

Category 1. Superficial complaints designed to send the message, "I'm not happy with this situation or with my partner." I usually conclude that these scenes have been ongoing, and they are often not actually addressing the real issues.

Category 2. The underlying issues, usually repetitive and conflictual in nature, actually have not been identi-fied and openly discussed. Possibly, these issues are due to unsolvable problems.

Category 3. Important and specific needs that each partner has that have not been openly stated or fully satisfied, and unresolved hurts that have lingered on for a long time. Possibly, there are unhealthy issues with origins in the past of one or both partners.

Possible Solutions

- Tell your partner honestly what you feel, need, and want.

- Don't attack or criticize your partner; use your skills to attack and solve problems together.

- Don't be a martyr, and don't keep things in and suffer; it builds resentment and resolves nothing.

- Open your heart, let your guard down, and be vulnerable with your partner to reach true intimacy.

- Share your dreams and fantasies, and you can be sure that your partner will do the same.

- Let your partner know and feel your love; you may not feel safe, but you will feel well connected.

- Pride does not belong in a loving relationship; let your pride go and admit your insecurities.

- Ask yourself, "What is the real problem that I am trying to solve?" rather than "Who can I blame for this problem?"

- Ask yourself, rather than asking your partner, "What can I do to make the relationship better?"

- Listen to the silence in your relationship; that usually speaks volumes about what's wrong.

50. The Problem: Feeling Unhappy? Talk Now!

So you have committed yourself to a relationship, and perhaps you married your partner. Things were going well for quite a while, and you and your mate were satisfied, although both of you slowly recognized that there were thoughts, feelings, and behaviors that were causing problems in the relationship. In my opinion, this is the most crucial time in a relationship, because so many couples choose not to confront these difficulties and instead allow them to fester, creating emotional disconnections, major conflicts, and possibly infidelity. Sadly, the average couple avoids dealing with major difficulties in their relationship for as long as six years. But each partner may conclude that the real problem is not him or her, and instead think that, "If only my partner did what I want, we would have no problems." I promise you, I have never treated a couple whose difficulties were due to only one, not both, of them—although the contribution may not always have been equal. I strongly recommend that couples confront whatever difficulties they are facing head-on.

Possible Solutions

- Ask yourself honestly, What are the problems that I want to solve? What has been my contribution to creating them?

- Make a few dates, preferably outside the house, and at that time, quietly and honestly talk to each other.

- Schedule an appointment with your religious leader, and be completely open to listening.

- Find and meet with a psychologist with expertise in couples therapy if the above steps failed.

- Utilize couples therapy effectively; avoid the cycles of accusations and counteraccusations.

- Honestly accept and work on eliminating your active contributions to the ongoing problems.

- Identify, write down, and discuss the most important needs you both have and want satisfied.

- Accept that neither you nor your partner will have all your needs fully satisfied.

- Don't waste time in therapy focusing on past problems; they are not changeable. Stay in the now.

- Stay realistic in your demands, expectations, and future possibilities; accept what's possible.

- Commit completely to the effort of improving the relationship; otherwise, you're wasting time.

- Don't make the therapist your judge and jury; work hard at following his or her recommendations.

51. The Problem: Identifying Co-Dependency

One of the major problems that I encounter in treating couples is the vicious cycle of "co-dependency" when there is an addictive personality or substance abuse in the relationship. It is common knowledge that those with addictive personalities often deny that they have a problem. It is also common knowledge that a person who abuses substances, gambles, or is a workaholic usually has a partner who tries to get them to control or stop those behaviors. When this pattern continues for a while, an additional problem, separate from the addiction, ultimately surfaces. The partner who has the problem, and often is in denial of it, rejects their partner's efforts and becomes angry at being told what to do. They then, consciously or subconsciously, repeat the same behaviors to prove that no one can tell them what to do. In turn, the individual who is the recipient of these addictive behaviors becomes more angry and insistent that the behaviors stop, often using logic and, at times, manipulation to achieve their goals. When this pattern becomes entrenched, a vicious and repetitive cycle takes place called "co-dependency." This problem becomes impossible to resolve, and can continue indefinitely until a tragedy occurs or a drastic action is taken by either partner. Many relationships have come to an end because of this problem.

Possible Solutions

For the partner who is dealing with an addictive personality:

- Accept the reality that nagging will accomplish the opposite of your desired goal.

- Realize that the only one who can stop these negative behaviors is your partner, not you.

- Know that you have control over only one thing, and that's whether to stay or leave.

- Review your own conscious and neurotic reasons that make you obsessed with a particular problem.

- Consider the possibility that the real underlying problem for both of you may be intimacy issues.

- Question why you keep repeating the same efforts in spite of not getting positive results.

- Understand that what your partner is doing is not to punish you, but instead to punish themselves.

For the partner with an addictive personality:

- Analyze what unhappiness you are compensating for in engaging in addictive patterns.

- Consider whether your behaviors are ultimately making you any happier or more satisfied.

- Question whether you have evaluated how different your life would be without the abuse.

- Consider the possibility that your actions are due to underlying fears of closeness and intimacy.

- Question whether you may be self-medicating, masking your anxiety and depression.

- Know that you will address your addiction only when you do it for yourself, not anyone else.

- Accept that you have the strength necessary to become the person you wish to be.

52. The Problem: Developing and Maintaining Emotional Intimacy

I believe that emotional intimacy is one of the most important goals that romantic couples should try to achieve. All of us struggle with two competing desires: to be emotionally safe and to feel emotionally connected to someone else. Different people have different levels of comfort regarding how vulnerable they are willing to make themselves. I think that intimacy is achieved at the high cost of opening our lives up completely to another person, allowing ourselves to be vulnerable and transparent enough to allow another to reach us at the deepest level of our being. This happens from sharing ourselves with our partners fully, and maintaining a deep level of honesty in sharing who we are physically, spiritually, intellectually, and emotionally. An intimate couple enjoys life together, feeling a sense of anticipation as they explore life's surprises together; they enjoy cherishing and being cherished, nurturing and being nurtured. Clearly, to accomplish intimacy we must be brave enough to be very vulnerable, while realizing that a rejection can be devastating. In a romantic relationship, "emotional intimacy" is considered the gold standard.

Possible Solutions

How to eliminate emotions and behaviors that are barriers to intimacy:

- Don't ever betray trust in your relationship; it takes a very long time, if ever, to gain it back.

- Don't fear openness when you have the opportunities to show and share it.

- Don't hang on too long to painful hurts and unresolved anger, and don't be too self-protective.

- Don't try to live a dual life, married and single; you have to fully commit to the relationship.

- Don't bring jealousy and criticism to a relationship and expect openness and vulnerability.

- Don't withhold love, affection, or sex by making it conditional on getting your way.

- Don't act with indifference and boredom toward your partner and expect the relationship to be close.

- Don't keep on bringing up old, unfinished business and assume that this time you'll resolve it.

How to increase intimacy:

- Be honest and open about your thoughts, feelings, and actions with your partner.

- Be respectful, affectionate, encouraging, supportive, accepting, and loving of your partner.

- Be thankful and appreciative of your partner's efforts, and verbalize these thoughts to them.

- Be willing to share your dreams, fears, insecurities, and desires with your mate.

- Be truly interested in getting a deeper understanding of your partner's dreams, fears, and wishes.

- Be open to your partner's views and influences, even when you are sure that your way is right.

- Be open to laughter during difficult times to lighten up the situation.

- Be accepting of your partner's mistakes, flaws, and limitations; remember, you're not perfect, either.

53. The Problem: Managing Anger

Anger is an inevitable part of any relationship. It is nearly impossible to live intimately without, at times, lashing out and hurting each other. Anger is neither right nor wrong, although the way we behave as a result of our anger can be viewed as either right or wrong. Anger is a very difficult emotion, whether you are on the receiving end or dishing it out. Sometimes anger can cause minor hurts, while at other times the injury can be quite significant, lasting a long time. Some couples try holding back their anger by suppressing or ignoring it, only to discover that their relationship becomes disconnected and cold, while resentments and unresolved emotional injuries accumulate. Other couples seem to freely let loose and express every single thought and emotion that they experience at the moment, causing significant hurt and damage which will then be recounted days, months, or even years later. Clearly, there are better and healthier alternatives; we can learn how to express anger in ways that do not cause unnecessary and destructive injuries. Anger is a secondary emotion that we usually express when we experience a primary emotion such as hurt, rejection, criticism, or abandonment.

Possible Solutions

When you are angry:

- Ask yourself, "Exactly what was I thinking and, perhaps, exaggerating that made me angry?"

- Identify the negative statements that you are telling yourself regarding the situation.

- Question the patterns and why you had these problems with your partner in the past; is there anything different?

- Analyze your intent when you decided to lash out at your mate; did you want to attack or defend?

- In the first ten seconds, before you react, decide how you want to express your feelings.

- Ask yourself: Am I willing to be vulnerable enough to share my hurt feelings rather than my anger?

- When you know you are too angry to face a problem rationally, walk away until you cool off.

- Analyze whether your anger has to do with not getting your way, rather than being hurt or rejected.

- Question whether you are arriving at conclusions without really understanding the situation.

- Are you mimicking your parents' behavior in expressing your anger and frustration?

- Remember that you have control over how and when you express your feelings of anger.

- Remember that what you think affects how you feel, which affects how you behave!

54. The Problem: Considering Forgiveness

In any relationship, there are many areas that can lead to conflicts, from the simple issues of what TV shows to watch to differences in parenting and complicated family problems. Forgiveness is an essential ingredient of any relationship, because hurt is a part of every relationship. I believe that when we decide to forgive someone, we make a conscious decision to let go of our feelings of resentment, regardless of whether that person actually deserves our forgiveness. Forgiving someone does not necessarily mean that we forget what was done, or deny what happened, or make excuses for that person. I think that the most important factor in forgiving someone is to ultimately set ourselves free from being prisoners of that person's actions, which can generate sadness and stress. I think we should forgive someone more for our own well-being than the other person's benefit; it sets us free. Of course, every effort should be made to discuss the area of conflict. Emotions should be openly shared, and efforts to share views with one another should be made.

Possible Solutions

- Be sure that you are not drawing conclusions based on assumptions; what are the facts?

- Be open to sharing your thoughts and feelings, and be sure to listen to your partner's views.

- Don't let anger drive your decisions, and try to honestly assess your partner's intentions.

- Ask yourself, What do I lose and what do I gain by forgiving and trying to renew the relationship?

- Challenge yourself to evaluate and admit your contributions to the problems.

- Know whether your unwillingness to forgive is due to stubbornness, revenge, pride, or just hurt.

- Think of the possibility that your reactions to the incident may be due to issues in your past.

- Question whether you are forgiving too quickly because you do not want to face the underlying problems.

- Know whether you are forgiving a wrong because you're willing and ready or because you're afraid.

- Don't expect that forgiving someone will make your feelings of hurt and resentment fall away; it takes time.

- Don't forgive on the assumption that you will have a great satisfaction or sincere apology from your partner; forgiveness is unconditional.

- Don't say, "I forgive you," and then spend time trying to punish and collect your pound of flesh.

chapter eight

PERSONALITIES, SEX, AND DISCONNECTION

*"It is amazing how complete is the delusion that beauty
is goodness."*

— Leo Tolstoy

55. The Problem: Knowing Personalities

Most people select a partner based on what they like about the other person's looks. Ultimately, we all fall into a particular personality type, which describes attitudes and behaviors we bring to the table in our relationships. I have often wondered whether the process of selecting a partner would change significantly if we had the luxury of a clear description of our partner's personality type. I want to offer a description of four different personality types that we most likely exhibit, and that show who we are. Perhaps by reviewing these, you will recognize and better understand the pros and cons of your partner's personality, and learn to deal with it more effectively.

Possible Solutions

Understand the four personality styles:

The Helper

The helpers are people who need people, and they love to be involved with others. Usually, they are well aware of the feelings of others, and are intuitive and empathic. In relationships, it is very important for the helpers to be seen as genuinely caring; they tend to be peace-makers, and work to obtain cooperation and harmony. The helper generally tends to see the positive in most situations and is loyal, trusting, and supportive.

They may be seen as: weaklings; pushovers; too easily hurt; lacking enthusiasm.

They need to learn to: confront others; say no; not feel responsible for others' happiness.

The Organizer

The organizers tend to be very responsible, and are almost always prepared to follow the rules. If something lacks structure, they strive to get it structured and organized quickly. The organizer is viewed as reliable, stable, and someone who ultimately gets things done. In general, organizers don't enjoy lots of change, prefer predictability, and tend to look to the past when making decisions. Among their major gifts are their sense of order and follow-through; they almost always tend to focus on completing their work, and consider pleasure only after everything is done.

They may be seen as: stubborn; perhaps too rigid; inflexible and unyielding.

They need to learn to: be less critical; be more diplomatic; be less demanding; reduce expectations.

The Thinker

The thinkers enjoy new ideas, analyze situations, and tend to be observers. They are independent, and are more involved with thoughts and ideas than with emotions. They follow the rules only if the rules make sense or are logical. The thinkers have a need to be competent and to accumulate knowledge. They enjoy discussions of ideas and a lively debate. They are great planners, even to the point of perfectionism, and they consider all the options before deciding.

They may be seen as: insensitive; too controlling; loners; procrastinators; sarcastic.

They need to learn to: avoid sarcasm; be less rigid; include others; be in touch with others' feelings.

The Catalyst

The catalysts enjoy being free, spontaneous, and playful. They are bold in their actions, like to be the center of attention, and tend to be risk takers. They get bored easily, they like making things happen, and they enjoy a challenge to the point of being impulsive. They find rules and structure confining, and are treasured for their spontaneity and outgoing nature. These are the fun-lovers to whom everybody is attracted in the short term.

They may be seen as: too unrealistic; too impulsive; lacking follow through; too dangerous.

They need to learn to: be more organized; not take too many risks; stop challenging authority; slow down.

56. The Problem: Valuing Sexuality in a Relationship

I first want to address some of the more general faulty assumptions about lovemaking. The first has to do with sexual desire. Recognize that just because your partner is attractive, it doesn't necessarily mean that you must desire them. One has nothing to do with the other. The second assumption is that men should have an erection if they are attracted to their partner. Again, if you are a man, just because you are attracted to your partner doesn't necessarily mean that you should automatically get an erection. The third faulty assumption is that lovemaking really means penis-vagina intercourse, and that anything else is deviant and unhealthy. In general, there seems to be discomfort in our population regarding sex, including talking about your needs openly with your partner, discussing openly what you want or don't want, and initiating the activity, even among couples who have lived together for a long time. Lovemaking is a very important part of a relationship, allowing the couple to develop physical and emotional intimacy, and every healthy individual benefits both physically and emotionally from it. Consider discussing the following questions with your partner.

Possible Solutions

- If you cannot get an erection, what's going on in your life that is stressing you out?

- Do you and your partner openly discuss each other's needs and desires in lovemaking?

- Do you or your partner ever withhold sex as a punishment, or because you're angry?

- Do you have sexual fantasies that you don't share with your mate, worried that they're not normal?

- What are your biggest concerns about your sex life with your partner; do you share them?

- Do you know what your partner likes and does not like during lovemaking; if you don't, why not?

- How comfortable are you with your body during sex; does your partner know about it?

- How concerned are you about sexually satisfying your partner? Do they know about it?

- How well do you know your and your partner's sexual anatomy, which generates arousal?

- How often do you worry about failure to maintain an erection?

- Do you kiss during lovemaking, and how often do you actually reach orgasm?

- Do you worry about what's "normal" or "not normal," and what you desire and fantasize about?

- Do you really know what you need for a totally satisfying sexual experience?

- Does your partner masturbate, and do you masturbate? Why or why not?

- Do you and your partner have the same amount of sexual desire? If not, what do you do?

- What do you usually think about before and during sex? Do you share it with your partner?

57. The Problem: Confronting a Relationship in Trouble

No two relationships are alike, and most couples seldom achieve a perfect union. We all know couples who have a successful relationship in spite of different family values, temperaments, or personalities. Similarly, there are couples who seem to be a perfect match, but somehow the relationship ends in failure. The mystery seems to have been resolved by research of the past few decades, carried out by experts in the field of couples counseling, which concludes that the answer lies in a couple's ability to master certain principles in dealing successfully with each other. In fact, a team of researchers at the Gottman Institute has been able to successfully predict, with 90 percent accuracy, when a relationship will end by identifying a set of "relationship destructive behaviors." The saddest experience for me is when I meet with a couple for the first time, and I am aware that they waited too long to seek help because they're not talking, not fighting, and not complaining anymore. If you and/or your partner engage in the following actions, you can be fairly sure that your relationship, sooner or later, will come to an end.

Possible Solutions

- Have you noticed that neither you nor your partner makes an effort at making peace?

- Do you and your partner often engage in criticizing each other's character or personality?

- Do you and/or your partner engage in defensiveness, that usually says, "It's not me, it's you?"

- Do you and/or your partner go silent, stop listening, and just tune each other out?

- Have you noticed that you or your partner engage in name-calling, sarcasm, or hostile humor?

- Have you noticed that when you talk to each other, there are many emotions and no resolutions?

- Do you see a lot of negative body language messages going back and forth at each other?

- Do you or your partner create opportunities to calm down, or suggest taking a break?

- Do you or your partner reject the opportunities and/or efforts to repair the relationship?

- Do you find that you or your partner only focus and talk about bad memories of the past?

- Do you and your partner make sure to go to bed at different times to avoid each other?

- Have you thought, or said aloud to others, that you have considered separation or divorce?

chapter nine

INFIDELITY

"It is not lack of love, but lack of friendship that makes
unhappy marriages."
— Friedrich Nietzsche

A Few Thoughts on Infidelity

Infidelity is a very important subject, and it requires a more detailed discussion. We first need to understand the stages of a romantic relationship before we try to understand the reasons for infidelity. There are typically four stages of a love relationship: the first is the "honeymoon phase," in which both partners feel passion and the desire for togetherness. The second stage is the "discovery stage," in which both partners realistically recognize their differences and are in conflict about them. The third stage is the "differences phase," in which couples work toward learning and accepting each other's feelings, thoughts, and differences. The fourth stage is the "acceptance stage," in which the couple has created an acceptable bond and a life together. They love and accept each other for who they are and are resigned to their unresolvable differences.

With only rare exceptions, infidelity tends to occur when the second stage of the relationship has not been fully resolved, and the couple engages in one of these two styles of conflict: the Avoidant style, where on the surface the relationship appears healthy and the two seem well suited, while underneath they are very fearful of confronting their problems; or the Dependent style, where the couple usually leads with anger without necessarily identifying, discussing, and accepting their feelings.

When the couple is unable to get past the discovery stage of the relationship, they are typically unable to overcome one or more of these possible emotional conflicts:

1. Years of accumulated anger, pain, and disappointment inflicted on each other.

2. Years of drifting apart, being disconnected, and killing love and intimacy by the refusal to deal with their differences.

3. The refusal, by one or both partners, to accept their contributions to the problems in the relationship.

When the couple has not gone through the second stage of the relationship effectively, has taken on a style of conflict, and has been unable to overcome one or more of the three possible emotional conflicts, sometimes infidelity is the outcome. There are many reasons why a partner may decide to have an affair, which include needing to prove their manhood or attractiveness, going through a midlife crisis, and refusing to accept the commitment to the relationship (wanting to be single forever).

However, the most recognized reasons for infidelity are the following three, which are assumed to be based on the following negative emotions:

1. **Fear.** Fear of intimacy, commitment, or being unworthy of love, leading to "reject before getting rejected."

2. **Loneliness.** Feeling alone and disconnected for a long time. When opportunities become available, like someone giving you time and attention, you will feel special and alive again.

Unfortunately, this means that loneliness has been accepted between the two partners, rather than dealt with or confronted, usually normalizing more unhappiness.

3. **Anger.** The irrational belief by one partner that the relationship should fulfill all their needs; or the desire for revenge for being hurt, rejected, mistreated, or abandoned. Finally, the use of anger for self-protection, in which a partner thinks, "I don't think I'm good enough for you, so I'm leaving you before you leave me."

Effectively treating infidelity in a romantic relationship most often requires couples counseling. The couple needs help going through all the stages successfully, and needs to follow a series of difficult steps as part of a lengthy process. The following suggestions are designed to help the process along toward a positive resolution when possible, rather than the ending of the relationship. The therapist will most likely focus on these solutions.

Possible Solutions

- Deal with the betrayed partner's devastation; assess for suicide, rage, sorrow, fear, homicidal ideation, and impulsive decision making. Define, for both partners, unacceptable behaviors and actions; allow emotions to be expressed, and help control the chaos.

- Determine the betraying partner's commitment to working on the relationship; assess for sincere commitment to a long-term relationship, answering questions to the other's satisfaction, engaging in delay tactics to keep options open, ensuring that the affair relationship is completely over, and guarding against impatience in allowing the betrayed partner to express and process all of their emotions.

- Evaluate the long-term infidelity issues and the love relationship; assess what stage the couple is in at the present time, the strength and intensity of the love, and the strengths and weaknesses of each partner. Evaluate the level of intimacy and the willingness of each partner to continue. Recognize any deal-breakers present, the openness to suggestion and compromise, and the ability and tendency to express affection toward each other (whether verbal, nonverbal, nonsexual physical, or sexual).

Note: It is highly recommended that if you are dealing with infidelity, you should find a well-qualified mental health professional to help you try to save the relationship.

58. The Problem: Infidelity Happened, Now What?

Nothing could be more devastating to a romantic relationship than infidelity, which violates the most basic principle of any relationship: trust. Yes, most often a relationship can develop and grow only when trust is achieved and maintained, making it the cornerstone to building commitment, intimacy, and love. I strongly believe that couples should make major commitments to try to save their relationship. I always remind couples seeking counseling due to infidelity that, regardless of the reasons, an affair is never, ever justified. I point out, though, that an affair is usually a significant symptom that the relationship is in trouble, and the cause(s) need to be uncovered and resolved. Infidelity does not have to destroy a relationship, and many relationships dealing with infidelity survive. Even an affair can ultimately be a great opportunity to build a wonderful, lasting relationship for the future. However, I also make it very clear that an "all-in" commitment by both partners, and a lot of work, are required for any future success. I believe that both partners can move from pain and regret to connection, love, and intimacy in the future. But they must understand and follow these suggestions.

Possible Solutions

- The betrayed partner must be heard and empathized with when sharing all their hurt and rage.

- The betrayed partner must have the right to mourn the loss of trust before moving forward.

- The betraying partner must be honest and transparent about their thoughts, feelings, and actions.

- The commitment to work on the relationship must be agreed upon by both partners.

- Contributing problems by both partners must be identified, acknowledged, and resolved.

- Important needs requested to be met by each partner should be identified and discussed.

- Communication between the partners should be open, intimate, supportive, and honest.

- The time period for the process is decided only by the betrayed partner, no exceptions.

- Trust by the betraying partner will have to be earned with honest efforts over a span of time.

- A prerequisite to building an intimate, long-lasting, and loving relationship is vulnerability.

- Forgiving by the betrayed partner can occur with lots of work, but you cannot be sure they will forget.

- Understand that the relationship, for better or worse, will never be the same.

59. The Problem: Deciding to End the Relationship

I always tell couples, "I believe in marriage, I am pro-marriage, and my goal is always to help you save your relationship. However, I am not 'pro-misery,' so if you cannot improve the relationship, then you should try to dismantle it with the least amount of pain and destruction possible." I hate to admit that, more often than not, I have failed miserably in achieving a peaceful dismantling of a relationship. My first goal in dealing with couples ending their relationship is to find ways to protect the children. Every opportunity I get, I remind one, the other, or both to leave the children alone and keep them out of their emotional conflicts. Unfortunately, I don't always succeed in accomplishing that goal, either. Often, in a divorce the children are the real victims and pay the highest price. Whenever possible, I help couples understand that the real battles in dismantling their relationship have to do with hurt feelings and bruised egos, which usually turn into a "revenge" mode, especially if infidelity was the main reason for ending the relationship. Unfortunately, most couples are not truly aware that the real factors to be negotiated, when ending a marriage, have clear guidelines. Any issues can be resolved easily and efficiently among themselves and their respective lawyers, rather than going through the extremely expensive and difficult court process. It is important to note that many people later regret having initiated a separation and divorce. They often realize that they still had loving feelings for their partner, in addition to having to deal with all the changes and struggles they now have to face alone. If you have decided to end your marriage or relationship, think about the following questions.

- Are you sure that you have really tried everything you could to fix the relationship?

- Do you have the financial resources to live apart from your partner, and can you handle the financial changes after divorcing?

- Have you really tried to make significant changes in your thoughts, attitudes, and behavior?

- Have you really communicated clearly to your partner what you are unhappy about?

- Do you have a clear sense of what your life will be like once you have gotten divorced?

- Have you really thought about how the divorce will affect your children and other family members?

- Exactly what can your partner do to make you want to stay in the relationship at this point?

- Have you evaluated how realistic your expectations of a reasonable marriage were?

- Have you honestly assessed your major contributions to the failure of the relationship?

- How well do you think you and your partner have communicated about each other's needs?

- Do you believe you have found a new "soulmate?" (Second marriages fail 70 percent of the time.)

- Know whether the reasons for ending your relationship are mostly emotional or mostly logical.

chapter ten

THE DIVORCE PROCESS

> *"The opposite of love is not hate, it's indifference. The*
> *opposite of art is not ugliness, it's indifference. The*
> *opposite of faith is not heresy, it's indifference. And the*
> *opposite of life is not death, it's indifference!"*
>
> — Elie Wiesel

A Few Thoughts on Divorce

Over the past forty years as a clinical psychologist, I have seen mature adults seem greedy, boastful, hateful, and even frightened during the process of divorce. People who have been loving parents and generous to a fault suddenly want it all, or don't stop certain behaviors that everybody knows are clearly hurting their children. While on the surface, the conflicts seem focused on money, their emotional volatility is really due to issues of separation, rejection, and loss, which are among the earliest and most painful recurring experiences in our lives. The idea of equitable and fair distribution is defined subjectively by one or both partners, often creating competitive and oppositional attitudes and behaviors. A divorce generates a multitude of emotions for all involved, usually connected to the underlying struggles.

The work of a mental health professional helping someone going through a divorce should focus on the following five emotional areas:

1. Unfulfilled Expectations, which create Disappointment and Betrayal. The goal in healing is to teach forgiveness.

2. Losses, which create Sadness and Depression. The healing process should focus on doing grief work.

3. Separation, which creates Anxiety and Panic. The best focus should give someone faith that healing can be achieved.

4. Competition, which generates Self-Interest and Greed. This is usually healed by reconstructing the values of the relationship.

5. Adversarial System, which creates Suspicion and Paranoia The focus of this struggle is to re-develop trust.

Yes, a divorce is a long, painful, and overwhelming process that significantly impacts the family and friends connected to it. Unfortunately, one or both partners, the lawyers, and the legal system usually further complicate every step in the process. Most people go into a divorce blindly assuming all kinds of unreasonable possibilities. While many divorcing couples threaten each other with outrageous actions, there are legal, clear-cut guidelines in place that should be followed. Additionally, one should be aware that judges are not usually interested in opinions, only in facts. Many of the legal issues described below have established standards and guidelines in place. Issues that do not have set guidelines are usually resolved based on previous, customary actions often practiced by lawyers. In an effort to provide the reader with a simple outline of the divorce process and the different issues that usually need to be resolved, I offer the following information.

Simply, these are the usual legal issues that most couples negotiate in a divorce process, in the form of questions that must be resolved:

1) Parenting Arrangements (child custody and visitations)

A. Custodial Parent: Which parent should have primary responsibility for the children, including residence and decision-making authority?

B. Joint Custody: Should the parent who has legal responsibility for the children usually confer with the other parent for decision making?

C. Visitation/Access: How much time should the non-custodial parent spend with the child?

2) Support Arrangements (child support and maintenance)

A. Maintenance (alimony): How much, and for how long, should a spouse receive financial support?

B. Child Support: How much, and for how long, should a parent pay for support of a child?

C. Insurance: How much and for how long should a party provide medical or life insurance for children and a spouse?

3) Division of Property

A. Equitable Distribution: What should be the division of the marital property and debts acquired in either or both spouses' names?

4) Taxes

A. Exemptions: Which parent should have the tax-exemption credit for the child?

B. Prior Returns: How should the spouses share responsibility for problems with previous joint returns?

C. Capital Gains: How should the parties share responsibility for capital gains taxes on marital property?

5) Grounds for Divorce

A. Cruel and inhuman treatment.

B. Abandonment.

C. Confinement (when a partner is imprisoned for three or more years).

D. Adultery.

E. Degree of judgment of separation (when the husband and wife have lived apart for a period of one or more years, with proof).

F. A formal written agreement of separation.

G. The relationship between husband and wife has broken down irretrievably for a period of at least six months.

60. The Problem: Managing a Divorce Well

Divorce is an emotional bomb exploding in a family and social system, leaving no one untouched. The destructiveness of divorce, which may be ostensibly focused on finances, is usually connected to hidden (or not so hidden) emotions that each partner ultimately experiences. I have spent a significant amount of time and energy in my practice trying to get couples going through divorce to think more rationally, behave more practically, and consider the consequences of their actions—for other family members, the children, their friends, and even each other. I have seen outrageous emotions and behavior from reasonable and loving human beings. I suppose that there are no limits when it comes to the affairs of the heart.

Possible Solutions

- Before you divorce, make sure that you are 100 percent sure and you have looked at all options.

- If possible, and if there has been no abuse or severe conflict, utilize a divorce mediator.

- If you are worried about negotiating effectively, meet with your mate and both lawyers.

- If a court process has started, insist that your lawyers get together and settle it.

- Don't get into arguments with your partner about the past and who is right or wrong.

- Use only email to communicate with your partner if you tend to argue each time you talk.

- No matter what, never badmouth your mate to family, friends, and especially children.

- Never use your children to communicate crucial information to the other parent.

- Remember, it doesn't matter whether your or your spouse has the children; you will feel resentful and cheated.

- When you have the children, you will feel resentful for the full burden of the responsibility.

- When you don't have the children, you will feel you lost them and the house but are still paying for them.

- Don't allow children to manipulate you if you're feeling guilty or trying to win them over.

- Don't buy your children's love to prove to them that you're the better of the two parents.

- Never undermine your partner's parenting or sabotage their efforts at discipline.

- Make sure that both you and your spouse let the children know that "it's not your fault."

- Never share with your children the negative reasons why the divorce took place.

- Always encourage your children to listen to and respect the other parent, no matter what.

- Before you take any legal action, ask yourself, "Is what I'm doing fair or a punishment?"

- Remember that if you are dissatisfied with the divorce settlement, it was probably fair.

- Don't push a new partner on your children before they are emotionally ready.

61. The Problem: Telling the Children About the Divorce

In spite of what most parents believe, children are aware of everything that is going on in the family. When I did family therapy, I always asked for a session alone with the youngest child, who would fill me in on the issues and personalities of each family member and the roles that each individual played. Unfortunately, children are not privy to the reasons why their parents are acting the way they are, and they often end up drawing their own, often distorted conclusions. Young children don't have the maturity to conclude that Mommy and Daddy are upset, or are acting strangely because there is something wrong in their lives. What they often do conclude, and unfortunately end up blaming themselves for, is that the parents must be upset with them because they have been "bad" or are doing something wrong to upset them. Young children even start misbehaving because they conclude that they are what their parents think they are. At times, when children suspect that their parents are not getting along, they start acting out and getting into trouble so that the parents will have to get along better and join forces to deal with them.

The following are some constructive steps on what to tell the children about your decision to divorce.

Possible Solutions

- Don't say anything to the kids until you are very sure that you and your partner are divorcing.

- Don't lie to the kids, don't make up stories, and don't go into elaborate explanations.

- When you talk to them, do so together, with no personal details and no accusations.

- Allow your children to express their feelings without belittling or dismissing them.

- Before you and your partner talk to the children, agree on what to say and how to say it.

- No matter what your partner says during the talk with the kids, don't argue or debate.

The following outline should be a useful list of things to say to the kids about your decision: a. You have probably noticed that we haven't been getting along with each other lately. b. We really don't love each other anymore the way people who stay married love each other. c. You know that we love you very much. Parents always love their children; that love never changes. d. This decision has nothing to do with you, and there's nothing you could have done to stop this. e. This decision is between Mom and Dad and it's not your fault, even when we argue over you. f. Dad/Mom is going to move, and you will spend time sometimes at my house, other times at Dad/Mom's. g. You should know that most things will stay pretty much the same, like school, friends, and family. h. But some changes do happen. When you are with me, we'll do things and go places without Dad/Mom; when you are with Dad/Mom, you'll do things and go places together without me. i. In a way, we kind of have two families, two houses, two sets of activities, and two places to be. j. This is nothing to be embarrassed about; you can tell your friends or anybody else you want. k. When you are finished, ask the kids, "Do you have any questions?" l. When you are asked "Why?" or "Which one of you wants the divorce?" the answer should be something like: "This is something that we have thought about a lot, and we feel this is the best thing to do."

62. The Problem: Divorcing Without Destroying

The divorce process can be lengthy (one to four years, on average) and difficult. Each partner, regardless of who initiated the divorce, is overwhelmed by emotions and a flurry of difficult changes to adjust to in a very short period of time. If your partner wants the divorce, you question your attractiveness, attitude, and actions that may have driven the other person away. If you are the one who initiated the divorce, you question whether you made the right decision, worry about what family and friends are going to say about you, become concerned about losing your connection to your family, and grow fearful of what the future will bring. Finances take the spotlight fairly quickly because the same amount of money will now have to support two domains, and the quality of life will have to be re-adjusted downward; a fear of making ends meet often becomes overwhelming for most people. If infidelity is the cause of the divorce, you as the betraying partner will have to deal with the anger and judgment that will surely follow once the information becomes public. Both partners in a divorce are often clueless about the legal process and may get advice from friends who have gone through a divorce, family members who are very angry, or confusing and incomplete information from lawyers. This onslaught of data can cause additional worry and confusion.

Because of all these and many other issues, people may lose the ability to think logically, practically, and reasonably. Therefore, the following list of actions and attitudes should be monitored quite carefully.

Possible Solutions

- Don't rush and start dating just because you feel lonely, insecure, or scared; it's not helpful.

- Don't blame yourself for not being beautiful, manly, or rich enough.

- Don't blame everything on your partner, no matter how upset you are; in most cases both partners contributed to it.

- Don't look for ways to punish your partner; recognize that revenge is a double-edged sword.

- Don't try to "buy" your children and your spouse to compensate for your guilt; it's damaging.

- Don't commit to another relationship too quickly; take your time to process all your emotions.

- Don't demand, bully, or bribe your children into accepting your newfound soulmate too early.

- Don't criticize your partner to your children and family; they are still your child's parent.

- Don't allow yourself to become too dependent on your kids, family, and friends.

- Don't make major decisions during the early periods of the divorce; they may be costly.

- Don't ignore the reality that your financial status will change; consider your options carefully.

- Don't make your children your allies against your partner, or your own personal confidants.

- Don't go around collecting opinions from everyone; make your own decisions.

- Don't follow any legal advice blindly; when all is said and done, be your own legal advisor.

- Don't allow your emotions to be the most influential factor in your decisions; most of the time, use logic.

63. The Problem: Divorced But Still Connected

Unfortunately, when marriages come to an end, the venom and animosity between the two former partners may remain unabated, which strangely keeps the two connected. Neither is then able to move on and create a new life. When children are involved, these destructive patterns continue to impose misery on them as well. For such couples, to create two separate worlds and develop separate family systems sometimes remains impossible. Underneath these behaviors, one can easily identify fear, loneliness, regret, and an unwillingness to forgive both oneself and the partner. The fear of the unknowns of the future, the loss of a family unit, the regrets over what each contributed to the ultimate failure of the relationship, and the unwillingness to forgive all make people unwilling to let go of the past and move on. Yes, almost every spouse who has gone through a divorce is able to provide a long list of unfair and unreasonable things the other partner may have done before, during, and after the divorce. However, this list is usually used to rationalize and justify the continuous destructive patterns in a relationship that ultimately ended a long time ago.

What are some healthier actions that you can carry out in your life once the divorce is over?

Possible Solutions

- Accept responsibility for your contributions to the destructive patterns that ended the relationship.

- Create a detailed plan for yourself and your children of what you wish your future to be.

- The plan should include details about family, friends, work, self-improvement, and romance.

- Evaluate and change your views about finances, parenting, relationships, and the roles you play.

- Forgive everyone you're angry at; this is a great gift to give to yourself, even more than to others.

- Your detailed plan is your guide; however, stay in the moment and take one day at a time.

- Always focus all your thoughts on what you can do, rather than what you can't.

- Mourn your losses: the life you had, your friends, your family, and so on for a time, then move forward.

- Look at your future as an opportunity to create and become, rather than fearing the unknown.

- Use your past as a guide to lessons learned, and work hard to avoid repeating the same mistakes.

- Seek guidance only to get additional information; make your own decisions.

- Remember, you are a lovable and good person; you deserve to make yourself happy.

PART IV

Career: From Training to Retirement

chapter eleven

THE CAREER

> *"Success is not final, failure is not fatal: it is the courage to continue that counts."*
>
> — Winston Churchill

A Few Thoughts on Selecting a Career

Henry David Thoreau said, "Most men would feel insulted if it were proposed to employ them in throwing stones over a wall, and then throwing them back again, merely that they might earn their wages. But many are no more worthily employed now."

Many Americans today are unhappy with their jobs, and yet a culture of careerism has led full-time workers to spend a huge amount of their day at work. Moreover, it's rare for people in today's workforce to truly match their natural skill set to their job. Adding further complications to the problems of career selection and job satisfaction are the educational institutions in our country, which continue to graduate large numbers of students without regard to whether there are jobs available in their particular field and/or whether these graduates are uniquely qualified for the field they have selected. All that together equals a borderline crisis of work.

It is quite amazing that despite living in such a progressive nation, with brilliant minds running our national and educational institutions, we have not yet developed more effective methods of matching people to what they are best qualified to do in their careers.

It would be extremely useful if we could:

- Make lists of the natural and learned skills needed for specific careers.

- Select objective, reliable, and valid tests to evaluate these skills.

- Test high school seniors before graduation to help choose careers based on these results.

- Create realistic educational/vocational tracks based on the identified strengths of these students.

- Have colleges and trade schools develop programs based on the job demands of the time.

- Have corporations and businesses offer hands-on training and internships for these graduates.

- Have such programs nationwide, and evaluate and modify them regularly as needed.

While I am not qualified to address any of these problems, in the following pages I will offer some ideas, suggestions, and directions that may help you better navigate your career path. Hopefully you will discover something about who you are, what you are good at, what you think you like to do, how it should be done more effectively, how to seek a career in which you may succeed, and how to change your career for a more satisfying and successful alternative.

64. The Problem: Considering Important Factors in Selecting a Perfect Career

Achieving success in selecting an appropriate and satisfying career requires a comprehensive assessment of different personal factors.

Unfortunately, many people are not aware of, or do not take the trouble to learn about, their strengths and weaknesses and how these factors might affect their career. The goal is to decide what you want to do with your life and make a concerted effort to create a career step by step. It takes a certain amount of effort and courage to be the author of your own future—turning your dreams into reality, struggling through when you feel stuck, and managing uncertainties. The process requires asking significant questions, looking from within, and seeking answers from the external world, often struggling with the possibility that you will not get the answers and will have to make them up. Sometimes decisions are difficult to make, and you'll have only yourself to count on and trust. A serious commitment to the process is a prerequisite to achieving your goal, recognizing that when you are tired and you want to give up is when you must push yourself harder and further, until you feel confident that you know what to do.

The following proposals should be reviewed, analyzed, fully understood, and carried out.

Possible Solutions

- Find out what you want, need, and desire from your career to be satisfied.

- Ask yourself if you have the passion and commitment to search for all the answers.

- Evaluate how your present situation limits your possibilities, and what to do about it.

- Find out who you are: your personality traits, limitations, and temperament.

- Objectively evaluate and learn about your skills, abilities, and natural or learned talents.

- Search for and identify your meaning, mission, and purpose in life.

- Be sure to aim high, go after everything you want, and believe that you can do it all and well.

- Forget the past; create your future from the present forward with no fear.

- Analyze what makes you unhappy, frustrated, and sad in your present career.

- Be sure to match your skills, abilities, personality, and desires to your career.

- Make a list of six possible careers that seem to match your needs, skills, and desires.

- Go through each career on the list, make a list of pros and cons for each, and choose one.

- Once you have selected a career, be sure that you acquire all the required qualifications.

- Seeking a job in your career of choice requires a series of important activities, including:

  - Writing an exceptional resume that makes you stand out from the rest of the crowd.

  - Learning and applying the most effective techniques of personal marketing.

  - Making your job hunt a project, a job that you commit yourself to every day.

  - Making a list of all the people who can possibly help you, and rating them, A, B, C, or D with regard to their value in helping you.

- Developing more personal relationships when networking, and contributing to them with each interaction.

- When asking for help or a job, being straightforward, confident, and honest.

65. The Problem: Considering "Intelligence"

We often conclude that someone is intelligent because they do very well in school. There are multiple tests utilized to measure intelligence, and unfortunately, many children in the school system are pigeonholed according to these measures. Based on the individuals' academic success and intelligence scores, many children and adolescents end up feeling discouraged and often are made to feel inferior to other students. Often, this is also true about adults, who are judged based on their history of academic success. Sadly, we fail to prove to each individual that they possess a unique combination of abilities that the world has perhaps never seen before, one they can use to create new things, develop new thoughts, and apply to new purposes in life. I am sure all of us can think of dozens of people who have shown unique talents when doing certain things, leaving us totally impressed with their exceptional skills. So we need to be careful in how we judge people's intelligence, in case we end up labeling children, adolescents, and adults unfairly, especially since such labels can cause significant and permanent damage. Define who you are above and beyond what you have accomplished academically, or the degrees you have acquired.

Possible Solutions

- Never allow someone to judge or criticize you based on your skill set.

- Identify and utilize your own unique strengths in practical ways.

- Never take people seriously when they compare you to anyone. You are uniquely you.

- Discover your unique abilities as early as possible and quickly put them to work.

- Don't waste time trying to develop your weaknesses; instead, sharpen your strengths.

- Know that no one is better than you at everything; you do have your own special skills.

- Separate "who you are" from "what you do." Some things you do well, others you don't.

- Remember, you have the power to either define yourself or have others do it for you.

- Know that perfection does not exist, but you should always strive for improvement.

- Know and accept your limitations, but don't let them define you as a person.

- Who you are is developed from the inside out, not from other people: the outside in.

66. The Problem: Knowing Your Natural Skills and Abilities

Success and happiness at work, and perhaps in life, may well be based on identifying, developing, and utilizing a person's natural skills and abilities. Everyone is born with a unique set of talents that are as individual as their fingerprints. However, literally millions of people live their lives with their aptitudes and natural skills lying dormant within them, while feeling stuck and quietly suffering in careers that don't fulfill them. Few people are in a truly appropriate job for them, and even fewer fully utilize their natural and learned skill sets. Even those people who recognize and identify their natural and learned abilities still don't necessarily know how to accurately identify the careers that will best maximize their potential. Unfortunately, most people who are already in the middle of their career will find any change to be very difficult. However, if you are extremely unhappy in your job, or are a high school or college student just embarking on your career path, you should consider the following suggestions seriously.

Possible Solutions

- Think about what you're passionate about and what comes easily to you.

- Meet with your guidance counselor and ask to evaluate your vocational interests.

- Before graduating high school and choosing a college, assess your natural skills and abilities.

- Choose a college and a major based on a career matching your validly measured abilities.

- List what you believe your natural and learned abilities are at this time in your life.

- Ask people who know you best what they think your strongest abilities are.

- Take the ability tests available on the government website O.net.

- Find a career counselor who offers specific testing on your abilities and matches them to different careers.

- If you are passionate about something and don't know enough about it, go and learn.

- Don't assume that if something comes easily to you, it's not really a talent; it usually is.

- Remember that you can always improve on any skill that you are passionate about.

67. The Problem: Knowing the Important Skills for Job Success

Some studies have sought to identify what skills and abilities are best matched to different careers, and there is a consensus as to what skills are most important for success in any given field. With progress being made in more objectively assessing human beings' natural and learned skills, we now have opportunities to better understand and utilize these skills for success in the workplace. But it is important to realize that what one may enjoy may not necessarily line up with what one is best suited for.

The following abilities and skills have been assessed as important factors to be identified when trying to find a successful match for a particular career, and should be objectively evaluated by qualified professionals.

Possible Solutions

- Intelligence (IQ) refers to thinking skills, and is one of the most important global skills required to succeed at work and in life. The IQ test measures inductive reasoning, deductive reasoning, analytical reasoning, vocabulary, memory, visual motor coordination, and other skills. An up-to-date intelligence test administered by a qualified psychologist will provide you with useful information regarding your skill set.

- Emotional intelligence (EQ) is the ability to know and manage both your emotions and the emotions of others—very important skills in most careers, especially those that require effective communication and ongoing interaction with others. This is a learnable skill!

- Personality plays a major role in the career-selection process.

There are many different tests available that match your personality to the best careers for you, and create profiles that range from the comprehensive to the superficial. Have a qualified psychologist administer such a test.

- Vocational Interest tests are designed to help you identify the field to which you are most attracted. Remember that these tests do not evaluate whether you are qualified to do the job you like.

- Verbal Reasoning is the ability to think abstractly, analyze deeply, and find common ground among different concepts. This is an important skill in achieving success in most careers, especially those in which communication is crucial.

- Abstract Reasoning is the nonverbal ability to identify common patterns within information, effectively solve problems, and make strategic choices. This skill is important for many careers, especially ones that involve decision making.

- Mechanical Reasoning is the ability to understand machinery, tools, and the concepts behind them. This skill is very important for people who choose careers involving physical forces and mechanical concepts.

- Numerical Ability refers to the understanding of numerical operations and relationships, and the ability to compute and calculate with numbers. A very important skill for careers in accounting and finance, among others.

- Spatial Relations is the ability to visualize objects and patterns three-dimensionally and try to imagine what they would look like if rotated in space. Successful architects, engineers, and draftsmen score very high in these skills.

- Language Usage is the ability to detect errors in grammar, punctuation, and capitalization. The ability to write effectively and correctly is quite important in most careers, especially those that require strong communicators.

There are very sophisticated tests designed to evaluate the skills listed here, as well as many other skills including vision, drive, judgment, adaptation to change, planning and organizing, resilience, teamwork and collaboration. There are also other measurable, specialized skills, including manipulating objects skillfully, remembering sounds, learning languages, and more. If you are looking to obtain a comprehensive assessment of all your natural and learned skills, make sure you find a qualified professional or agency that can provide you with an appropriate assessment. Remember that knowing your strengths, what you are really good at and what comes naturally to you, will help you select the best and most appropriate career, which will significantly improve the probability of being happier and more satisfied at work.

chapter twelve

THE CAREER AND THE SEARCH WITHIN

"The secret of success is making your vocation your vacation."

— Mark Twain

68. The Problem: Searching Within Oneself in Selecting a Career

Perhaps building your future career should start by first posing a series of questions to yourself that have to be honestly and practically answered. This process will help you recognize what you need to clarify, what you need to learn, what your responsibilities are, and what steps need to be taken to achieve your desired goal. Once you define your career goals, specifically outline what your job should satisfy in terms of needs, comforts, rewards, and general values. Additionally, the goal should include your hopes and dreams for the future and an effort at satisfying yourself. As stated earlier, the search should always start from the inside out, so get to know yourself well. Try not to get stuck in dreaming about an idealized concept of a perfect career; be optimistic but practical. At the same time, seek to satisfy a sense of purpose. Be sure that the career has a meaning for you, and outline a mission statement of what is important for you, because that's what will drive your enthusiasm and a sense of passion. The question, "What am I doing with my life?" should not be followed with "Who can I ask for a job?" but rather "What goals do I want to satisfy in choosing my future career?" There is a clear difference between having a job and developing a career.

Please consider addressing the following questions, and try to answer them with total honesty before selecting a career.

Possible Solutions

- Do I have a clear sense of my personality traits and temperament? Do they fit my choice?

- Have I clearly defined my values, mission, and purpose as they apply to a career?

- Am I really willing to push myself through the limits to accomplish what I have outlined?

- Am I clear about my sense of purpose, and will the career I am selecting satisfy it?

- Have I thought about all my other wants and responsibilities before choosing this career?

- Do I have clarity about the settings, people, and philosophy of the place where I will work?

- Am I ignoring major needs, feelings, values, costs, or consequences in selecting this career?

- Have I made a full commitment to building a solid foundation for my future career?

- Am I excited and passionate about the work I am going to do?

- Have I tried everything and ignored nothing before deciding on the present career?

- Am I making careful decisions in building my career future one block at a time?

- Does the idea of going to work at my job make me anxious, bored, or very excited?

69. The Problem: Knowing Who You Are

Very often we make wrong assumptions in concluding that we truly know ourselves. Many of us don't have a clear sense of what we are like, and don't understand our complex personalities and predispositions very well. Realistically, other people in our lives know us better than we know ourselves, and often when they try to share some of our shortcomings with us, we become dismissive or defensive. There are some really sophisticated and objective personality tests that can define our strengths and limitations, and others that measure how these strengths and weaknesses will affect our performance at work. Even a small mismatch between your personality and your job can make going to work much less pleasant, or even miserable. While many of our personality traits are inherited, we can still effect change in our thoughts and behaviors. However, it's still best to match your personal strengths to your career rather than working hard at trying to improve on your limitations.

Possible Solutions

- Have both your work skills and your personality tested by a professional.

- Learn about and understand the major components of your temperament.

- Ask others their views of your personality.

- Honestly analyze your own attitude and personality traits.

- As best as you can, look for ways to change any of the areas requiring improvement.

- Try to change your attitude from a "glass half empty" to "half full."

- As often as possible, work hard at being an optimist; always look for the silver lining.

- Look at what makes you comfortable so you can match who you are to what you do.

- Don't be seduced by money or power when choosing a career; remain who you are.

- Make an honest list of all the strengths and weaknesses in your personality and attitude.

- Try to evaluate how these factors are a match or a mismatch with your career selection.

- Remember the adage, "If it looks like a duck, walks like a duck, and quacks like a duck, it's a duck."

70. The Problem: Analyzing and Comparing Different Careers

This is a great exercise for you to further discover the benefits and drawbacks to different careers and find out which are as close as possible to being a perfect fit with everything that is important to you. Choose half a dozen possible careers that you believe are practical and possible for you. Once you've come up with a great list, making sure they're as different from one another as possible, begin to compare and contrast each with the others. Make sure that you do this exercise in writing, and include as detailed description of these careers as possible. Try to describe the most valuable benefits that each career can offer you, including how such a career will make you feel, what a typical workday will be like, the different activities surrounding this career, and what skills and abilities you will be utilizing when working at such a job. As honestly and realistically as you can, describe what each career would be like for you.

Make sure to be as comprehensive as possible.

Once you have finished this process with each of the careers you have selected, carry out the following steps.

Possible Solutions

- On the top right side of each career you have written down, write "very good" or "not so good," with a line separating the two. Find all the positive things about each career that you can come up with, considering all the possible aspects of the job and asking as many questions as possible. Then write them down under "very good."

- For each career, carry out the same exercise and write down all the possible things that you find to be "not so good" on the other side. Be just as critical as you were in seeking the positives, and give it significant thought by asking important questions about issues that you find not pleasing to you.

- When you have completed the exercise for each career and collected both the "very good" and the "not so good," create a list for each category, and out of these factors, decide the twelve most important factors you deem "very good" and the twelve most important factors you recognize as "not so good."

- Now go back to each of the careers you selected, and compare and contrast them in terms of the "very good" and "not so good" factors. Select the career that seems to include the positive factors most attractive to you, and look for patterns that make a few alternative choices attractive as well. This analysis should be extremely helpful in selecting a career.

chapter thirteen

SELF-MARKETING

"The higher we soar, the smaller we appear to those who cannot fly."

— Friedrich Nietzsche

71. The Problem: Writing an Effective Resume

Whether or not a resume is powerful often depends on who's looking at it. This section is not designed to offer complete details on how to write a superior resume. What I hope to accomplish here is helping you recognize the steps you can take to get the opportunity to be called in for an interview. I suspect that the goal of any resume is ultimately not to get the job, but instead to get an interview with the hiring manager. In turn, getting an interview with employers requires that one is able to get the attention of the individual who goes through the mind-numbing task of reviewing hundreds of resumes. Your opportunity to get recognized and, ultimately, selected for an interview requires that you do not write a resume that is a carbon copy of everybody else's, and somehow find a way to get the reviewer's attention and interest. A good resume should effectively let the prospective employer know that, if they choose you, they will get their important job requirements satisfied. So an exceptional resume depends on the ability to impress the prospective employer, so they will call you in for an interview and you can convince them that you have what it takes to successfully satisfy the requirements of the position.

Possible Solutions

- Do some research on the layout, format, and structure of a great resume.

- Recognize that the main focus of any good resume is the Objective section.

- The Objective should summarize how you will satisfy the employer's job needs.

- In the Objective, you have to demonstrate that you are the perfect candidate.

- Be simple and specific in selecting a few special qualities and abilities that make you stand out.

- Keep in mind that you are basically writing advertising copy for your best skills and abilities.

- You must identify the employer's needs, not yours, and state how you will satisfy them.

- Don't make the mistake of thinking that your resume is a written history of your past.

- Your resume will only get a ten-second scan, not a full read. Make a powerful statement first.

- Your resume should be about how effectively you can do the job, given your abilities.

- While your job history is required as well, the Summary section should be about your talents.

- In the Accomplishments section, select the most important highlights stated earlier.

- The worst mistakes of a resume: spelling errors, poor writing, and self-centered attitude.

- The order of a resume:
    1. Why you are the best candidate for the job
    2. Matching the employer's job requirements to your skill set
    3. Job history
    4. Education
    5. Summary

72. The Problem: Networking for Your Career

The concept of networking within a group for the sake of gaining acceptance or a benefit seems to create discomfort in most people. The bad news is that marketing yourself is often a necessary evil to get a job you want. Further, the traditional approaches to job hunting are very ineffective today, and the only way to ultimately get the job of your dreams is to effectively market yourself. Networking depends on many factors: who you know, how close a given person is to you and your family, your qualifications for the position, the demands of the job market, and your level of comfort in marketing yourself. Most of us are uncomfortable when asking for help out of a fear of rejection and humiliation. We are driven by the desire to feel safe, be correct, feel good, and avoid painful situations. All of these human desires are threatened to the core when we contact people for the sake of getting a job. Yes, marketing ourselves may sound like an uncomfortable and personally threatening activity that one wants to avoid. However, networking doesn't have to be uncomfortable if we take certain steps and remain true to certain principles.

Possible Solutions

- First of all, be sure to do everything possible to be proficient at the job you are seeking.

- Be upbeat and have a positive attitude about the job search, rather than being gloomy.

- Connect with those who can help you by giving of yourself and being generous.

- The most important part of networking is to create an honest friendship with others.

- Present yourself in the most favorable light: dress well, have a sharp resume, and smile.

- Make a job out of looking for a job. Create a structure and a routine to follow daily.

- Every industry has its own subculture; familiarize yourself with it and become part of it.

- Learn as much as you can about the industry; get to know people, get in the inner circle.

- Recognize the common threads within your industry and try to agree with others' views and positions.

- Make a list of your best assets, abilities, and skills, and make sure others notice them.

- Make a comprehensive list of everyone you know who could possibly help you get a job.

- Prioritize that list of the people you know from most to least important contacts.

- Contact each person, and be assertive, open, and direct in asking for what you want.

- Carry out activities that will help you be better prepared to connect with others, such as: a. Learning everything you can about your new field. b. Taking creative steps to try to get into the inner circle of people in the know. c. Creating a network of people who are in the same field. d. Learning about and attending conventions, seminars, and meetings in the field of interest. e. Volunteering your services and expertise for individuals and organizations in the same field. f. Being fun, positive, caring, and attentive, and engaging in reciprocity with others.

73. The Problem: Being the Best Employee You Can Be

Any employee can be trained to do their job effectively. However, you can't train someone to be honest, have self-confidence, be positive, or have a work ethic. You, as an employee, can bring the best or the worst of yourself into the workplace, and can make your job either a satisfying endeavor for yourself and others or a quiet state of ongoing misery. So much of what you bring into your job is totally under your control; the typical employer has no difficulty firing a bad employee or appreciating a great one. The most difficult employee is that person who tends to do an average to mediocre job while causing discomfort, frustration, and hopelessness for their supervisors and employers, who may be unhappy but cannot justify firing the person. So before you start a job, or after settling down into a new job, ask yourself, "What kind of employee do I really want to be for this company?"

The following list includes some of the qualities, traits, and behaviors that are globally valued by most managers and employers. You may want to evaluate the unique characteristics that you could bring to your job. Select from this list if you're not sure.

Possible Solutions

(Ask yourself, "Are these qualities I have, and do I bring them to the job?")

- A strong work ethic. I set specific goals and carry them out as requested by my employer.

- Dependability. I can be counted on to consistently follow through on my responsibilities.

- Self-motivation. I can be self-sufficient and responsible, with little direction from others.

- Positive attitude. I can be upbeat and fun, and I can create a good working environment.

- Effective communication. I say what I mean, and I understand the benefits of being clear.

- Team-oriented. I try to work well with others, and I make the most out of collaboration.

- Leadership skills. I use my leadership skills effectively if need be.

- Organizational skills. I am well organized when managing or carrying out assigned projects.

- Action-oriented. I am able and willing to take chances and generate ideas.

- Ambition. I strive to achieve personal success, while striving daily for results at my job.

- Success. My goal is to succeed at everything I try, and my work history shows it.

- Honesty/authenticity. Whatever else I strive for, I remain honest and forthright at work.

- Modesty. I don't usually brag about myself; I try to show my expertise through my daily work.

- Passion. Yes, my salary is important, but I'm passionate about the work's end goals.

- Creativity. I work at being proactive in solving problems and creating solutions at my job.

chapter fourteen

RETIREMENT

"People take different roads seeking fulfillment and
happiness. Just because they are not on your road doesn't
mean they've gotten lost."

— Dalai Lama XIV

74. The Problem: Are You Being Put Out to Pasture?

The word "retirement" means different things to different people, and it generates a flood of emotions ranging from excitement to confusion to panic. I believe retirement offers us an opportunity to finally live the life we want, since we have the freedom to do it our way at a time when we have the least amount of responsibilities and demands on us. It is strange that so many people plan their many stages of life in minute detail, and so few have no significant plans for their retirement, with the exception, perhaps, of their financial planning. We tend to forget, especially today when people live much longer than they did in the past, that retirement is really a stage of our lives rather than the end of life. During this stage, we can create a whole new life, a whole new career, or a new, uncharted path with a different lifestyle for many years. If retirees fail to give themselves a sense of purpose and a new path after their work life is done, they can become depressed and adrift. So it's important to create activities, something similar to "camp for grownups," in order to provide socialization, exercise, and a purpose in life. It is strongly recommended that, if you are planning to retire soon, you give some serious thought to what you're going to do with this next stage of your life. Whatever you are going to do, make sure that you research it well, and make sure that it will give you satisfaction!

Possible Solutions

- Look for opportunities to work as an independent consultant related to your old profession, either for a contracting firm or even your previous boss.

- Consider working part-time for your present employer, or take on special projects to carry out independently for the company.

- Start your own business regarding something you're passionate about, and be pleased to be your own boss.

- Look into starting a whole new career that you have wanted for a long time.

- Phase into retirement by slowly working less and less at your present position, ensuring that you are happy and comfortable.

- Take time off, maybe a year, to do all the things that you promised yourself you would do, and then select one of the other options listed.

- Whatever you select, look to satisfy desires that you couldn't accomplish when you needed to work.

- Offer your time and skills to a not-for-profit or community organization, utilizing your specific skills to help those in need.

- Under no circumstances allow yourself to do nothing and let your mind and body go into a state of perpetual vegetation until you die!

PART V

Friendship: From Acquaintances
to Best Friends

chapter fifteen

FRIENDSHIPS

*"Friendship is born at that moment when one man
says to another "'What! You too? I thought that no one
but myself..."'*

— C. S. Lewis

A Few Thoughts on Friendships

There is absolutely no question that friends are important no matter who you are. Having friends can be extremely beneficial to everyone, emotionally and even physically. Without friendships, we can feel extremely lonely to the point that our immune system is damaged and we get physically sick. "Feeling" isolated can be more dangerous than "being" isolated. In other words, it's not whether you're alone that affects your health; you can feel terribly isolated when you are around other people as well. The bottom line is that social isolation can lead to depression, physical illnesses, substance abuse, and even suicide.

Friendships do not happen automatically, although as humans we want to belong and need to be connected to others. Of course, we have to be careful not to idealize friendships to the point that we believe them to be all-satisfying and all-encompassing, without the inherent problems that accompany them. There are questions that must be confronted regarding friendships: How they should happen? What are they supposed to be? Whose fault is it when friendships are missing? What does it take to develop friendships? Should true friendships cause pain and disappointment? It should be clear to everyone that not all friendships are the same. They vary from simple acquaintances to best friends. Finally, we need to recognize that friendships can change in status, need to be accepted for what they are with honesty, and should be recognized based on our, not the friend's, experiences.

All of us ultimately need to confront our need for friendship, how many friends we actually have, what we are trying to satisfy in our friendships, and what our true circle of friends really consists of at the present time. We all ultimately need to define the level of closeness and intimacy that we are seeking, and assess whether the person we are seeking it from can deliver. Can we be less than fully satisfied with the friendships we do have?

Finally, you need to have the skills to develop friendships; understand why you don't initiate that process at times; develop methods to build and maintain trust; learn to manage fears of rejection; and engage in activities to ensure that the relationships you do have will ultimately survive in the long run.

75. The Problem: Not Having Friends Can Make You Sick

Not only is having friends a great pleasure in life, it is good for us—for our emotions, our minds, and even our bodies. Unfortunately, as adults, forging and maintaining friendships has become more difficult, causing loneliness and isolation. Some of the reasons for this problem include changes in social status due to divorce, people moving more often and further away, more people not having marital partners to supply the intimacy they need for long periods of time, and that everybody's life seems to be busier now than ever before. Personal networks have shrunk in recent years—see Robert Putnam's classic Bowling Alone, which details how the American sense of community has been undermined—and people seem lonelier than ever. Finally, individual perceptions of how socially satisfied we are add to the problem, suggesting that if we feel isolated, regardless of whether or not we are actually isolated, we can experience the same loneliness that often leads to depression and medical problems. For the sake of our emotional and physiological well-being, we should try hard to develop friendships.

Possible Solutions

- Get actively involved and become familiar with the same group of people over time.

- Take the important step, even if it is uncomfortable, of turning acquaintances into friendships.

- Take a chance and divulge personal secrets; this has been shown to be the best way to make friends.

- Accept that, while being rejected is painful, it is ultimately not fatal.

- Don't make excuses for yourself and say that friends don't matter; we all need friends.

- Don't assume that you will always be approached; you have to reach out and approach.

- Don't engage in self-fulfilling prophecy, convincing yourself that people don't care about you.

- Try to be genuinely interested in other people, rather than coming off as scared or self-centered.

- Cautiously use social media to share parts of yourself and connect with others.

- Don't create an internal panic and forge just any relationship; look for who makes you happy.

- Don't define your worth based on the number of friends rather than the quality.

- Don't judge yourself or others on the basis of how many friends you or they have.

76. The Problem: Having a Lot of Friends

Realistically, how many friends do we actually have? Many Americans, living in a society that values independence and individualism, have almost no close friends outside one relationship, typically their significant other. How many friends do we actually need? Most of us have one or two confidants in our close circle, but ideally we would be happiest with three to five "committed friends." So it's useful to analyze friendship a bit more deeply.

It has been suggested that there are five levels of friendship. From the most distant to the closest, they have been described as:

1. Contact friends

2. Common friends

3. Confirmed friends

4. Community friends

5. Committed friends

Try to analyze your five circles of friendship and find out which friends best fit in which of the five categories. It is also useful to recognize when friendships fail to satisfy our needs.

Possible Solutions

- Remain consciously aware when your friendships are shifting; you may be forced to accept a new status.

- Be sure to separate your desire for possible friendships from the connections now available to you.

- Don't be seduced by other people's feelings and desires; remain aware of your own feelings and be true to yourself.

- Accept that being chosen as a friend doesn't have to be an exclusive process; both people can have other friends without jealousy.

- If you think everyone is your friend, you have failed to develop deeper friendships; the truth may be that you have no friends.

- There are times you need to accept that a friend is not really meeting your needs right now, and you need others for support.

- In life changes or crises, you may need someone who understands your specific situation, and perhaps even your best friend may not be that person.

- No one friend will ever meet your every emotional and social need; it is useful to accept their limitations, and that's why we need a circle of friends.

- Developing intimacy requires a major emotional commitment on both sides.

- Evaluate your needs and requirements for a successful friendship.

- Honestly evaluate whether your expectations of your best friend(s) are realistic.

- Trust your relationship; allow your committed friends the freedom to enjoy others.

77. The Problem: Creating New Friendships

The worst thing you can do is begin to question the intentions of people who could possibly become friends. You could analyze their comments, actions, or attitudes and draw negative or wrong conclusions. This is especially true if you focus on the possible negative motives that could be attributed to their actions. Often we fail to evaluate our own insecurities when questioning whether we are being criticized, rejected, or accepted and appreciated by others. It is quite amazing how we can create all kinds of negative scenes in our minds, convincing ourselves that we are absolutely correct in our analysis of a situation, then follow through by taking destructive actions that terminate opportunities for possible friendships. Many times, we don't allow ourselves the opportunity to develop a new friendship purely on the basis of feeling uncomfortable, or drawing wrong conclusions although nothing bad really happened.

There are many things you can do to initiate activities that will lead to developing new friendships. The following are some examples.

Possible Solutions

Actions to avoid in initiating opportunities for new friendships:

- Making excuses that you are too tired or too busy to seize a good opportunity for friendship.

- Not initiating opportunities with someone because you think the feelings aren't mutual.

- Wrongly concluding that someone is too good for you or you are too good for them.

- Protecting yourself and waiting out of fear until the other person initiates the process.

- Assuming that the other person is not interested in you, so you just don't initiate.

- Convincing yourself that you cannot be friends with someone because you have nothing in common.

Actions to initiate new friendships:

- Seek opportunities to present yourself as positive, friendly, and upbeat.

- Don't make excuses; accept that you want and need friends, so go after it.

- Start conversations by noticing and talking about things valued by the other person.

- Don't make small talk and let opportunities die; suggest something to do together.

- Be specific when making plans, don't be vague; directly say, for example, "Let's have lunch Sunday."

- Try to be more personal and intimate in the questions you answer or ask, and be sure to share yourself openly.

- Don't stand on social rules; reach out again, and don't assume disinterest in the other person.

- Be generous with your time, offer opportunities, and help with anything you can.

- Use your friendships and connections with friends to meet and connect with others.

78. The Problem: Developing Best Friends

Developing a best friend relationship requires that we commit ourselves for the long run, allow ourselves to fully trust another human being, and be vulnerable enough to create a significant level of intimacy. It takes a lot of time to develop a level of mutual comfort that can make us feel fully understood. Ultimately, our ability to grow through the five stages of friendship depends on both friends' predisposed personality traits, the amount of exposure we are willing to create between ourselves and the other person, the amount of openness and care we show each other, and the level of desire each individual experiences to make the relationship succeed. Best friends' relationships don't happen without awkwardness and hurt feelings at times. This type of relationship demands that we support each other at the most difficult, demanding, and messy times in each other's lives, always remembering to follow the unspoken statement, "I will always be there for you."

The following steps are the usual path to achieve the best friend relationship.

Possible Solutions

- The definition of a best friend starts with responsibility, bonding, and trust in each other.

- To develop a best friend requires time, consistency, and mutual effort.

- Most friendships start with feelings of wanting to know more and talking to each other.

- The "want to know" feelings drive us to spend more time together and explore possibilities.

- The friendship grows slowly through multiple exposures to generate familiarity.

- In becoming more familiar with each other, we are more willing to be vulnerable.

- True vulnerability generates a sense of trust, which usually leads to being open and honest.

- When trust develops, we allow ourselves to let our guard down and create intimacy.

- Most of the time, true intimacy is ultimately what the best friend relationship demands on a regular basis.

- To summarize, the process of developing a best friend follows these steps: from curiosity, to exploration, to familiarity, to vulnerability, to intimacy.

79. The Problem: Developing Intimacy

The best way to get close to someone is by allowing ourselves to share the most vulnerable parts of our lives. But it is human nature to hide the worst of ourselves from others and try to present the best to everyone. The strange phenomenon of getting closer to someone by sharing the worst and most vulnerable parts of ourselves with them seems to suggest the following steps to intimacy:

Step 1. We decide to share something personal and vulnerable with someone.

Step 2. The other person is relieved to hear that we are opening up, sharing vulnerable parts of ourselves, and trusting them with something very personal.

Step 3. That person then makes the decision to share something personal and vulnerable about themselves, feeling safer to trust us because we trusted them.

Step 4. Both of us feel safer, trusting each other enough not to be concerned about being negatively judged, criticized, or rejected. Allowing ourselves to appear vulnerable with someone else allows them to be vulnerable with us as well, creating closeness.

Vulnerability leads to emotional intimacy, which often leads to friendship. So how do we express vulnerability and deal with the fears behind it? The following list offers some ideas.

- We must have the willingness to be comfortable with who we are, accepting and liking ourselves.

- We must be willing to accept our limitations and flaws.

- We should try not to be critical and judgmental of other people.

- We need to share vulnerable parts of ourselves in order to achieve more closeness.

- We need to be willing to face fears of rejection.

- We need to be willing to blindly trust another human being.

- We sometimes have to be the first one to reach out.

- We have to accept hurtful actions by the other.

- We have to be forgiving of others' painful treatment.

- We have to be willing to keep sharing, even when others don't.

- We have to be willing to keep on giving to the other.

- Finally, we must accept the ultimate, painful rejection.

80. The Problem: When Problems Surface in Friendships

No relationship, regardless of its level of intimacy, is trouble-free forever. There are certain common problems that tend to surface in friendships, which can either make or break a relationship if not carefully handled. Some of the difficulties may be created by our own perceptions and expectations, while others may be real; in either case, we need to decide how to handle them. Let's face it: we are all human, with needs, neuroses, unrealistic expectations, and faulty perceptions. We also have the distortion in thinking that tells us that the "right thing to do" is the "thing that we would do in the same situation," without recognizing that not everyone is like us. In order to function effectively in our relationships, we must accept differences between people, forgive transgressions, have realistic expectations of others, and hold ourselves responsible for our contributions to any problems. Most important, we must be committed to the responsibilities imposed on us by what friendships require to function well. We need to accept that no friend will ever satisfy all of our needs, and recognize that each friend may also bring some negatives that we must decide whether we are going to accept in order to preserve the relationship.

The following are some of the most common problems and Possible Solutions faced in friendships.

Possible Solutions

1. The Problem. At times, because we all compete, we experience resentment or jealousy toward our friends rather than being happy for them.

The Solutions. Understand that the jealousy is our problem, not our friend's. We need to recognize and be grateful for what the friendship offers, rather than stew over the ways our friends may be superior. It's useful to question the source of the jealousy—what is truly missing in our lives?—and the accuracy of our perceptions.

2. The Problem. Sometimes we confuse our views and opinions with facts, and proceed to impose expectations and judgments on friends who view things differently than we do.

The Solutions. Most important, we must accept people for who they are and give them the right to carry out their lives in the way that they see fit. We need to face that sometimes we want to impose our will on others to ensure that we are not wrong in how we manage our own lives. It scares us to be different from others. It's best to trust our friends as well as ourselves, and not make judgments.

3. The Problem. When we struggle, sometimes we feel like a friend is not truly there for us, and we become resentful and disappointed in them.

The Solutions. First, we must be careful not to assume that our friends are mind readers. We have to specifically ask for what we want. Second, we must recognize that our friends have lives of their own, and they are not necessarily ignoring us; they may just be busy.

4. The Problem. We may resent that we are on the giving end of the relationship and not getting a fair amount of reciprocity.

The Solutions. It is important to evaluate honestly what you do receive from your friends. Maybe you really don't feel important enough, and you're looking for evidence that your friends value you. Maybe you are a caretaker, and you just keep on giving whether the other person needs it or not; perhaps you are giving too much.

5. The Problem. Sometimes we experience negative feelings about ourselves when we are with our friends and conclude that they are just not good for us. They make us feel bad!

The Solutions. The first step is to evaluate whether your feelings are justified because you have a friend with a toxic personality. If so, you need to ask yourself, "Why have I selected such a friendship?" You also need to evaluate whether you view yourself as a victim of not only one particular friend but perhaps many other friends. Be sure to be honest with yourself, first and foremost, before taking action.

81. The Problem: Dealing with Negative Consequences and Loss of Friendships

In friendships, like all other relationships, situations can develop that lead to very painful and upsetting outcomes for those involved. Sometimes destructive actions and unfixable hurt feelings can lead to the end of a friendship, even your best friend. But often, significant efforts can be made to address and resolve such a situation without jeopardizing or terminating the relationship. Unfortunately, pride, strong egos, and the inability to be forgiving often make repairing the relationship almost impossible. Sometimes, the individual who is hurt struggles with and ultimately accomplishes the goal of forgiving, which brings peace to both parties. At other times, the party who caused the injury is able and willing to offer the sincere and necessary apologies that lead to rebuilding trust in the relationship. Unfortunately, sometimes friendships suffer irreparable damage or experience major changes, which leads to the termination of the relationship.

When faced with the possibility of a relationship coming to an end, it is useful to consider the following steps before, during, and after the problems surface.

Possible Solutions

- Honestly ask yourself, "What was my contribution to the problem?"

- Honestly review whether you did everything possible to save the relationship.

- Be absolutely sure that what you are reacting to or upset about is a real issue.

- Be sure that what you are being accused of is not based on rumors.

- When hurt is caused or experienced, give some time for introspection and healing.

- Be sure to allow some latitude; consider other possibilities about the incidents.

- Create an opportunity to express yourself honestly, without anger and accusations.

- Give your friend the opportunity to express their feelings without your being defensive.

- Value the relationship, and don't allow pride to cloud your judgment.

- Express feelings and thoughts using an "I" statement, rather than the accusatory "you."

- Don't debate your friend's feelings and thoughts; accept and empathize with them.

- Be empathic with the other person, rather than judging them.

- Seek resolution of the problem rather than debating it or defending yourself.

- If you made the decision that the relationship is over for you, just say so.

- Be prepared to mourn the loss of the relationship, and accept the pain that you can be sure will follow.

chapter sixteen

CONCLUSION: THRIVING IN LIFE

In the previous pages, I have addressed many of the problems that can cause people significant unhappiness and mental health difficulties. For each of these problems, I have offered a list of Possible Solutions to help you improve or manage them. I hope you found this information useful and are able to utilize it to improve your quality of life.

In conclusion, I want to share some difficulties that I have encountered, observed, wondered about, and struggled with in dealing with patients during my professional career. I have chosen these particular issues because they have surfaced continually in my practice, and I have struggled with them, often without clear resolutions, in my efforts to fully understand and manage the complexities of human nature. This list is not all-inclusive, and I am sure that I could come up with enough examples to double or triple it. But I want to share these difficulties, and my concerns, frustrations, and possible suggestions that could help you if you are dealing with them.

1. People don't change easily!

I don't think it's a surprise that changes are difficult for all of us. However, I have often been totally surprised by clients who refused to make the changes necessary to resolve a difficulty or significantly improve their quality of life. Strangely, while they may have whole-heartedly agreed with the suggested changes, they ultimately refused to make them in spite of being confronted with significant negative consequences to their behavior. I will admit that I have never fully understood these clients' resistance to change. I will also admit that I have often been disappointed in myself for my failure to encourage and convince them to try harder. In all honesty, this particular problem has been one of the most frustrating and unresolved struggles in my professional career.

As a final effort, I strongly recommend to anyone who struggles with a difficulty and is aware of Possible Solutions that they are refusing to take to please evaluate the reasoning behind those destructive decisions. If you recognize that you're one of the people who tends to reject changes, ask yourself: (a) What is it about these changes that stops me from carrying them out? (b) Is there a part of me that is looking to be a martyr and suffer unnecessarily, or am I secretly punishing someone close to me by my refusal? Finally, I suggest that you try harder to take the steps and make the changes that may improve your life. Albert Einstein said, "The measure of intelligence is the ability to change."

2. People tend to look too closely to clearly see the solution!

Sometimes we get so involved in the irrelevant details of a particular problem that we lose sight of the most obvious solutions or, worse, some of the positive aspects of the situation. I have often used my hand as a prop to help clients recognize the struggle of getting caught in minutiae. I point out that if they hold their hand too close to their face, they're limited to just looking at the lines on the palm and fail to see the whole hand, the totality of the situation. I remind them to step away enough to see the total picture of the problem more clearly, without the confounding emotions.

To anyone stuck in a circular pattern of reviewing the details of a problem, I recommend that you step back, give yourself the right to feel all of your emotions for a little while, and then engage your-mind by asking yourself: (a) What is the problem here? (b) Have I looked at all the pros and cons as objectively as possible? and (c) What are my best, most logical choices, options, and solutions? Most important, be honest with yourself.

3. People need to know the difference between "I will try" and "I will do it."

I am totally convinced that when we say to ourselves or others, "I'm going to try," we give ourselves a subtle and subconscious excuse to change our minds. We give ourselves an "escape clause" to utilize if we don't feel like doing something because it's too difficult, or we just don't feel like confronting it. I believe that the escape clause is totally eliminated when we say to ourselves or others, "I will do it!" The difference between those two statements is quite significant. If we say that we WILL do something, if it's not done, we are faced with an internal turmoil, a cognitive dissonance, that we find difficult to cope with. If we say we'll TRY to do something, no one, including ourselves, can really challenge how hard we actually tried.

My suggestion is to pay closer attention to which of the two statements you are utilizing whenever you are faced with a diffi-cult task requiring action: "I will try" versus "I will do it." I suspect you will be quite surprised to discover how you may be subtly lying to yourself.

4. People don't always know the difference between "unwilling" and "unable."

This problem has surfaced thousands of times in my practice, espe-cially when dealing with parents or spouses whose expectations regarding what their child or partner should be expected to do were not being met. We know that there are many tasks, behaviors, and activities that require some basic skills for a human being to carry out effectively. Some of these skills are simple enough, and most people assume that if a task is reasonable, the individual should be expected to do what is required without question. Unfortunately, most people just don't ask this simple question when expecting someone to carry out a responsibility: "Is this person truly able to do this particular thing?" If we are honest with ourselves, deep down we really do know the truth, even if we don't necessarily want to face the reality about someone's abilities and our unrealistic expectations.

I strongly recommend that you review your expectations of the people around you, especially close family members, and then, as honestly as possible, review people's abilities to actually meet them. Are your expectations reasonable? I truly believe that if you are honest with yourself, you will know whether a particular person is unwilling or unable to actually do what you expect, and deep down, you'll know whether you are being unreasonable. I encourage you to be accepting and forgiving of those people who are unable to meet your expectations, even when it is difficult. Especially when dealing with children, I suggest that you be more accepting, and focus on complimenting them on what they can do well rather than criticizing them for what they are unable to do.

5. Parents should pay attention to young children's symptoms of depression and anxiety!

During the first sixteen years of my practice, I treated children as young as four years old, and to my amazement, I discovered that a minority of them do truly suffer from severe anxiety and depression. I have treated children as young as seven who were able to describe, in clear detail, their plans to commit suicide. With rare exceptions, the majority of the depressed children's difficulties were connected to something going on in the family. If I am honest with myself, I have to admit that I stopped treating children younger than eleven years old because I was often frustrated and angry at their parents for their insistence that I "fix their child's problem" rather than demand that they change their own behavior. Most parents did not believe that young children could be depressed or anxious, and many refused to accept the role they may have played in their children's emotional difficulties. It is important to understand that children do not show symptoms of anxiety and depression the same way as grownups, so parents often fail to recognize the problem.

My first recommendation to parents is to learn about the many symptoms and possible consequences regarding depression and anxiety in young children. It is important as parents to pay close attention to changes in the child's sleep, eating, socialization, and moods and behaviors. If you suspect a problem, discuss this with the child's pediatrician, and if you get confirmation that a problem exists, ask for a referral to a qualified child psychologist.

6. People underestimate the power of the mind!

I am convinced that our minds are powerful enough to ultimately will us to live or die. I have observed this as a mental health professional too many times in my career to question it or take it lightly. I believe that too many people, too many times, don't use their mind's power to reverse their negative thoughts and behaviors, and instead resign themselves to unfortunate situations by giving in to their self-imposed hopelessness and helplessness. They convince themselves that they are totally unable to make any significant difference in their particular situation. In spite of the fact that every day we all observe the unbelievable tasks that people can accomplish when they make up their minds, we are capable of easily convincing ourselves to give up the fight. We allow our minds to convince us that there is nothing we can do, leading to a downward spiral causing further hopelessness and helplessness.

I have stated elsewhere, and it's worth repeating here, that we have the power to redirect our thoughts in ways that can strongly influence what we feel and what we do. If I could convince you that what I am saying is absolutely true, and further convince you that you should actually try to practice this simple concept, it would help you. The simple idea is: thinking positive thoughts causes you to feel positive, which leads to you act in more positive ways. Thinking negative thoughts causes you to feel negative and helpless, leading to achieving the negative outcome of self-fulfilling prophecy. The reverse is also true; doing something to help yourself usually makes you feel better, which makes you think more positively about your life.

7. Being defensive can be destructive!

I think that achieving self-actualization is ultimately based on our ability to honestly and fully accept our flaws and limitations, recognize and appreciate our strengths, and fully accept ourselves. None of us are truly comfortable with being made aware of our faults. However, we cannot grow and mature emotionally unless we are able to recognize and actively try to change certain attitudes and behaviors that can be destructive to ourselves and our relationships with others. I truly believe that only a strong individual is willing to be openly weak and vulnerable. I encourage you to be strong! In trying to help individuals or couples in counseling, my big struggle has always been to help them be less defensive, accept constructive criticism, and strive to change through self-awareness and feedback from others.

My recommendation to you is to remind yourself that to grow, you need to accept some constructive criticism so you can improve certain limitations in your personality, behavior, and attitude. I encourage you to be open and vulnerable enough to take whatever feedback you get and to consider it an act of love when those who care enough to help you grow offer you constructive feedback. Being defensive can be very isolating, and it interferes significantly with the ability to create closeness and intimacy. So be strong, be open to constructive criticism, be willing to grow!

8. People should accept the reality that the genetic predisposition does exist!

I will admit that I was confident, even arrogant, enough during the first four or five years as a mental health professional to think that any change is possible. I convinced myself that I was well trained, I understood human nature well, and I should not have any difficulties identifying the problems presented by my patients and offering them the appropriate solutions. Yes, I did learn about tension between "nature versus nurture," but I had my own ideas on the subject, and I concluded that if I understood a patient's problems clearly and motivated them enough, I could overcome the genetic influence and change them.

It took many years before I had to face the reality that there are some things—attitudes, behaviors, mannerisms, and even philosophies on life—that cannot truly be changed in a human being. I recognized, especially when doing family therapy for years, the powerful influence of genetic predispositions. Yes, I became quite convinced that a combination of the mother and father's gene pool played a major role in people's lives and, to a significant degree, an unchangeable role in human nature. I often told the complaining patients, regarding the failed expectations from someone in their lives, that "the person you're dealing with, and all that he or she brings to the table, is neither good nor bad; while it may be different, it is who they are. There are some things that people bring to the relationship that are part of their genetic makeup, and they are unchangeable." Over the years, I have become more convinced that genetics play a much greater role regarding how people are, how they behave, how they think, and how they feel.

My suggestion to you is to be open to the reality that your partner, friends, children, or siblings show significant physiological, emotional, and behavioral similarities to their parents and other family members. You must accept that many of these factors are unchangeable, a permanent part of the individual makeup. It's important not to judge but to accept that individual without labeling their actions as either good or bad. In the end, you must accept the good, the bad, and the ugly of those individuals' genetic predispositions if you are willing to have them in your life.

9. People do survive extreme levels of emotional suffering!

I have personally experienced, and have observed others experience, severe physical pain, and I am convinced that no matter how severe, this type of pain will never match an individual's emotional suffering. As a mental health professional, I have sadly witnessed the excruciating pain in the faces of parents who were mourning the death of their child. I have listened to people recount a sense of total hopelessness and sadness when dealing with the loss of a sibling, a husband, a wife, or a loved one. I have listened to the cries of people whose hearts were broken. At those times, I have often wondered how they would ever survive it, how they would ever move on with life, how they could possibly cope with such pain for a long period of time. But I have always been surprised by the resilience of the human spirit. I've always noted that with time, there was almost always a drive to survive and move on with life.

I want all of you who are suffering, or have suffered, from a painful situation to believe that your survival instinct will kick in no matter how devastating your emotional pain is at the moment. It's true that some losses or painful experiences may leave significant and permanent emotional scars, which ultimately become part of you and your life history. But we do go on—we must go on—in order to fulfill our destinies and live life to the best of our ability. You must believe that you have a built-in mechanism designed to generate enough strength and fortitude to survive. Again, to a significant degree, we owe it to ourselves and those we love to move on and become again an active member of society.

10. People do learn that small steps can lead to big changes!

Over the years, I have noticed how we tend to feel dissatisfied with whatever progress, success, or accomplishments we achieve in life. Often, we totally ignore the small successes, the small progress of things getting a little better. It's true that we need to strive toward goals and have a sense of purpose in life; however, it is also important to make our lives a journey rather than an obsession with the ultimate destination. In treating people who struggle with life's difficulties, I have found their inability or unwillingness to accept small changes to be a significant stumbling block to progress. I often encouraged them to appreciate their successes, no matter how small, to recognize that small steps are more likely to lead to permanent changes, and to understand that sudden and big changes are often temporary, leading to the possibility of sliding back and losing all the ground gained.

I encourage you not only to appreciate the small progress that you make in any endeavor, but also to reduce your expectations for the future, stay more in the moment, and try not to move too quickly. I have found that small steps ultimately are much more likely to lead to big changes in life, because we adjust better to easier, smaller, and less extreme changes. I also encourage you to make it a weekly habit to review and compliment yourself on any progress that you have made toward your goals, and appreciate all the other positives in your life.

11. People should learn that keeping it simple makes life easier!

I hate to admit how I wish I had taken more seriously the advice I received from the mentors in my life when they reminded me: "Keep it simple, don't blow things out of proportion, life isn't that complicated!" I truly believe I would have enjoyed my life much more if I had really listened and fully understood the importance of this simple advice. I have to thank my patients, who helped me recognize this problem in myself purely by observing them often making mountains out of molehills and significantly complicating their lives. I saw so many people create unhappiness and chaos in their lives over issues and problems that could have been easily resolved. I have often quoted the KISS rule—Keep It Simple, Stupid—to myself, to friends, to family, and to patients. Unfortunately, we as human beings tend to complicate the simplest situations by overthinking them, overanalyzing them, and talking them to death.

I want to suggest to you to heed that advice before you are well into the age of maturity. I promise you that the majority of the difficulties that you spend a tremendous amount of time and energy worrying about, being upset over, or complaining bitterly about, are either not worth it, can be resolved, or are unchangeable, and therefore all the energy is wasted. The best advice I can offer to help you avoid unnecessary complications is to ask yourself these simple questions: (a) What do I want? (b) Is what I want under my control? (c) Whether I act or not, am I willing to deal with and accept the consequences? Confucius said, "Life is really simple, but we insist on making it complicated."

12. My last suggestion to you: above all, respect yourself!

On the surface, this suggestion seems quite simple. Exactly what is it that we need to do to prove that we truly respect ourselves? I believe that most of us fool ourselves into thinking that we respect ourselves, that we are confident and competent, and sometimes we are even arrogant enough to judge others for their failure to be more like us. So, more realistically, what does self-respect translate into? I suspect that if this question was posed to a hundred people, the chances are we would get 150 or more different answers.

So I offer you my list from A to Z of what I always strive toward to fully accomplish self-respect:

A. Accept that you cannot respect yourself all the time; it's a daily struggle.

B. Respect your body by keeping it clean, staying well groomed, and trying hard not to abuse it.

C. Try to be who you are and say what you feel, regardless of others' opinions or approval.

D. Think for yourself rather than taking on other people's views.

E. Stop searching for the meaning of life and just live life as fully as possible now.

F. Speak when you have something to say, rather than saying something out of discomfort.

G. Don't force your wishes and opinions on others; help them think and then let them be.

H. Remain honest about your flaws and limitations, but work hard trying to reduce them.

I.   Always try to discover the limits of the possible, but try to push toward the impossible.

J.   Try to be fair, reasonable, and logical in your actions, and when all is said and done, be real.

K.   Work hard at trying to change yourself for the better; even a little every day is okay.

L.   Never make yourself unhappy by worrying about what other people think.

M.   Don't blame others, because you, nobody else, determines your destiny and your fate.

N.   Be clear and respectful to others in sharing your thoughts and feelings.

O.   Be courageous and generous enough to openly and honestly give of yourself to others.

P.   Treat yourself well before you give to others; otherwise, we all lose.

Q.   Recognize that you cannot be stepped on unless you allow it by lying down first.

R.   There is usually no real excuse for not being able to achieve your goals within your assumed abilities.

S.   Be careful with your prejudices; you know they are there, and you have to try to control them.

T.   Don't allow unrealistic fear or danger to keep you from achieving your goals.

U.   Never stop learning; realize now that you don't know what you don't know.

V. Never be fully satisfied with who you are; keep striving to re- create yourself.

W. Accept and appreciate the differences in others without being critical or threatened.

X. Never lose your identity for the sake of popularity.

Y. Never be overly dependent on others, nor allow others to be overly dependent on you.

Z. Never fear to lead if you know where you are going, and never fear to follow a great leader.

Yes, life can be complicated, unpredictable, and difficult for everyone at times. But throughout this book I have emphasized that we have a significant amount of control over how to manage life's difficulties, or prevent them from cropping up to begin with, by relying on certain skills or solutions that we can learn to implement.

The most important tools we have in managing our lives better are (1) to think more rationally and practically, (2) to behave more constructively, and (3) to recognize the power of our thoughts and actions over our emotions. Now that you understand the importance of these factors and you are able to practice the solutions I have offered throughout the book, I wish you good mental wellness as you incorporate these tools into your life so that you can **THRIVE, NOT JUST SURVIVE!**

Made in the USA
Middletown, DE
19 June 2020